HIGHLAND JACOBITES
1745

by
Frances McDonnell

CLEARFIELD

Copyright © 1999 by Frances McDonnell
All Rights Reserved.

Printed for
Clearfield Company, Inc. by
Genealogical Publishing Co., Inc.
Baltimore, Maryland
1999

Reprinted for
Clearfield Company, Inc. by
Genealogical Publishing Co., Inc.
Baltimore, Maryland
2002

International Standard Book Number: 0-8063-4935-2

Made in the United States of America

Introduction

In the Highlands of Scotland, where the Clan system operated and the tradition of unquestioning loyalty to the Clan Chief was still strong, raising and holding men in support of Prince Charles Edward Stuart's bid to wrest the throne of Britain from the House of Hanover - known as the Jacobite cause after the Prince's grandfather, King James - was not as troublesome as in the rest of the country. The following, to some extent, rescues from oblivion the achievements of the rank and file of the Highland Jacobite army, part of the cannon-fodder of the campaign.

The popular belief that in 1745 men flocked to join in the Stuart cause is unsupported by the facts; and, from the time of the Prince's landing to the fall of the curtain at the Battle of Culloden in April 1746, the Jacobite army fluctuated in strength and composition to an extent which makes it impossible to estimate with accuracy what the numbers were at any particular time. Many who were forced "out" took the first opportunity to desert, causing Lord George Murray, the leading Jacobite General, much anxiety. The expected English Jacobite support, so crucial, largely failed to turn out, but despite this the Jacobites got as far south as Derby, 100 miles from London, when a dispirited army, faced with three Hanoverian armies, went into retreat.

Willingly or unwillingly, in the knowledge of the inevitable consequences should they lose, the Scottish Jacobite leaders embarked on a course of armed resistance to an established Government equipped with a regular army well trained in warfare. Without the promised support of the French Government and the English Jacobites and opposed by the majority of their own fellow-countrymen, they set out on what was from its inception probably a Lost Cause; and a very large proportion of them paid heavily for their loyalty.

Due to the Hanoverian government's desire to identify each individual "rebel," court records, jail records, transportation orders and other documents were drawn up, rich in detail. As a result, more particulars on the ordinary man than is generally found are reproduced in this publication.

The failure of the '45 Rebellion began the eventual collapse of the Clan system, and within a generation large-scale emigration to North America was underway. To some it meant permanent exile from their native land; to all it meant physical and mental torture; to many, to far more than we can now say, it involved the painful journey to "Tir nan Og," from which there was no returning.

Frances McDonnell
St Andrews, May 1999

A HIGHLAND CHIEFTAIN

REFERENCES

Archives

PRO Public Record Office, London

    CO   Colonial Office
    SP   State Papers
    T   Treasury

SRO Scottish Record Office, Edinburgh

    GD   Gifts and Deposits

Publications

BMHS Barbados Museum Historical Society Journal
MR   *The Muster Roll of Prince Charles Edward Stuart's Army 1745-1746*
         A. Livingstone (Aberdeen, 1984)
P   *Prisoners of the '45*
         B. Seton (Edinburgh, 1929)
SHS   *List of Persons Concerned in the Rebellion 1745-46*
         Earl of Roseberry (Edinburgh, 1890)

HIGHLAND JACOBITES OF 1745

ANDERSON, THOMAS, Belmaduthie, Ross-shire. Servant to John McKenzie of Belmaduthie. Farmer. He is said to have "forced out several persons into the rebel service." This man submitted a memorial to the effect that he had never joined the rebels or taken any part, but was arrested "on the ill will of Neighbours," viz. one Lewis Rae. He further says he was induced to sign the petition for mercy and transportation. This petition appears to have been of no avail. Imprisoned July 1746 prison ship *Pamela* Tilbury. Transported 31.3.1747 to Jamaica 1747 on *St George or Carteret*. SHS.2.12, MR80, PRO.CO137.58, BMHS.30.74.

BAILY, WILLIAM, Glengarry's Regiment, aged 30 from Caithness, imprisoned Inverness, prison ship *Thane of Fife*, Tilbury, disposal unknown. SHS.2.18.

BAIN, DONALD, Glengarry's Regiment, Corimonie, Glenurquhart, Inverness-shire. "Forced the day before the battle of Culloden." Imprisoned in Inverness and Tilbury, transported 1747. SHS.2.18.

BAIN, DUNCAN, aged 30 from Ross, farmer in Glastollaigh. Cromarty's Regiment, imprisoned in Inverness, shipped on prison ship *Liberty & Property* to Medway. Transported 31.3.1747 from London to Jamaica in *St George or Carteret*, arriving Jamaica 1747. SHS.2.18, MR80, PRO.CO137.58, BMHS.30.74.

BAIN, DUNCAN, from Auchtine, Glenurquhart, Inverness-shire, Glengarry's Regiment. Surrendered along with the Grants of Glenurquhart at Balmacaan. Imprisoned 5.5.1746 in Inverness, his disposal is not traceable. SHS.2.18.

BAIN, JOHN, Glengarry's Regiment, from Corimonie, Glenurquhart, Inverness-shire imprisoned in Inverness and Tilbury, transported 1747 from Tilbury. *SHS.2.20.*

BAIN or BANE, KENNETH, Cromarty's Regiment, aged 24 from Ross-shire, imprisoned in Inverness and Tilbury Fort, servant to Daniel McLeod. At his trial was recommended to mercy. Transported 31 March 1747 from London to Jamaica in *St George or Carteret*, arrived Jamaica 1747. *SHS.2.20, MR80, PRO.CO137.58, BMHS.30.74.*

BARBER, DANIEL, from Inverness, imprisoned Culloden 16.4.1746. As his name does not appear again he probably died. *SHS.2.24.*

BATEMAN, KATHERINE, Keppoch's Regiment. Imprisoned on suspicion and released. *SHS.1.215.*

BEAN or BANE, DUNCAN, imprisoned Inverness and Tilbury. Transported 20.3.1747. *SHS.2.30.*

BEAN, GEORGE, imprisoned York Castle. Transported 8.5.1747 to Antigua. *SHS.2.30.*

BEANE, BENJAMIN, Cromarty's Regiment, aged 30 from Caithness, imprisoned in Inverness, and prison ship *Thane of Fife*, Tilbury. Nothing more is known about his disposal. May have died. *SHS.2.30.*

BEANE, JOHN, aged 22 from Caithness, imprisoned Inverness, prison ship *Thane of Fife* Tilbury, disposal not traced, may have died. *SHS.2.30.*

BEANE, KENNETH, Cromarty's Regiment, from Cromarty, imprisoned Inverness June 1746, prison ship *Jane of Leith*, Tilbury. Transported 20.3.1747 from London to Barbados in *Frere. SHS.2.30, MR81.*

BEANE, WILLIAM, McIntosh's Regiment, aged 30 from Inverness-shire, imprisoned in Inverness, and prison ship *Thane of Fife*. Disposal not known, may have died. *SHS.2.30.*

BEATON, ANGUS, Cromarty's Regiment, aged 48 from Caithness, imprisoned Inverness, and prison ship *Liberty & Property* Medway, prison ship *Alexander & James* Tilbury Fort. Miller to Laird of Ardglogh, Little Laids. Transported 31.3.1747 from London to Barbados in *Frere SHS.2.32, BMHS.30.74.*

BEATON, DONALD, from Island of Tiree, imprisoned Aug 1746 Tiree, 4.2.1747 Glasgow. "Was with ye rebels 2 or 3 days and knows not the Regiment." When examined he was found to be one of a group of men who denied being concerned in the Rising and who were guilty of habitual stealing. Discharged 15.4.1747. *SHS.2.32.*

BEATON or BEATING, JOHN, Sergeant, Duke of Perth's, from Inverness. Deserter. Taken at capture of Carlisle. He pleaded guilty at his trial and was sentenced to death, but was reprieved. He stated that he had been tried for desertion at Carlisle and condemned, but pardoned by the Duke of Cumberland. He appealed for release in February 1751 as he had not been transported. ? transported 1751. *SHS.2.32, MR68.*

BISSETT or VISSETT, WILLIAM, Lord Cromarty's Regiment, aged 30, farmer from Balmaduthie, Ross-shire, imprisoned in Inverness, prison ship *Wallsgrave* Tilbury Fort. Nothing more is known about his disposal. *SHS.2.36.*

BLACKIE, CHARLES, Kilmarnock's Horse Grenadiers, sailor from Campbeltown, Argyllshire. Imprisoned Campbeltown 2.6.1746, Dumbarton 7.7.1746, liberated 5.8.1747. "Joined the rebels at Edinburgh and continued with them till disperst." *SHS.2.38.*

BLAIR, THOMAS, feuar from Gartmore, imprisoned 9.5.1746 Stirling Castle and Carlisle. When taken prisoner he was found to have been shot through the arm. He was not brought to trial in September 1746 as he was "in hopes of being discharged for want of evidence." His name however is in the transportation list. Transported 21.3.1747. *SHS.2.38.*

BOWER or BOWYER, FRANCIS, aged 63, from Morar, imprisoned in Inverness and Tilbury. "A papist teacher of children." Transported 20.3.1747 from Tilbury. *SHS.2.44.*

BROWN, GEORGE, labourer from Innerwick, Groom to the Prince. Imprisoned in Stirling, released under General Pardon, 1747. "All the witnesses concur in saying he wore livery of the Pretender's son's grooms and acted as such." *SHS.2.52*

BRUCE, WILLIAM, aged 20 (30?), from Caithness, Lord Cromarty's Regiment, imprisoned in Inverness, prison ships *Thane of Fife*, and *Liberty & Property*, Tilbury. Husbandry in Dunbeath. Transported 31.3.1747 from London to Jamaica, in *St George or Carteret*, arriving Jamaica 1747. *SHS.2.56, PRO.CO.137.58, BMHS.30.74.*

BUCHANAN, JOHN, aged 20 from Argyll, "Stuart of Ardshiel's" imprisoned Culloden, Inverness, prison ship *Alexander & James*, Tilbury. His subsequent fate is unknown, probably died SHS.2.60.

BUCHANAN, JOHN, from Inverness-shire, Glenbucket's Regiment, imprisoned Culloden. As he does not appear to have reached London he probably died at sea. *SHS.2.60.*

BUIE or BUY, ANGUS, Craskie, Glenmoriston, Inverness-shire, Glengarry's Regiment, imprisoned Inverness and London. Transported. *SHS.2.60.*

BUIE or BUY, WILLIAM, from Ballindrom, Glenmoriston, Inverness-shire, Glengarry's Regiment, imprisoned Inverness and Tilbury. ""Pressed – a thief." Transported. *SHS.2.62.*

BURNETT, JOHN, of Campfield, Captain of Artillery, Captain, Col. Grant's, imprisoned 30.12.1745 Carlisle, London, Southwark. He is said "to have belonged to the artillery company at Woolwich." He said he was forced out by Glenbucket. He commanded the Carlisle Castle artillery. He fired the first cannon at the English army from Carlisle. He was taken prisoner at Carlisle on the surrender of the town, December 1745. He was sent to London, tried and convicted, but reprieved. Judge Burnett wrote to the Duke of Newcastle in his favour on 1 June 1747. He was pardoned 21 July 1748 and banished on condition of his not returning to the country. *SHS.2.64.*

CAMERON, ALEXANDER, SJ, The Revd Father, from Strathglass, Inverness-shire, imprisoned July 1746 Morar, July 1746 HMS *Furness* or *Furnace*, died at sea July 1746. Third son of John of Lochiel and brother of "Cameron of Lochiel" of the '45. He was a Jesuit priest. It is not known what part he took in the Rising. When taken prisoner he was put on board the *Furnace*, (Captain Ferguson), where he was allowed no bed to lie on, except cables. He fell ill and Lord Albemarle ordered him to be put ashore. Ferguson refused to give him up without an order from the Duke of Newcastle. He also refused to allow any bedding or clothes to be supplied to him. Cameron died soon after the ship arrived in the Thames. *SHS.1.224, SHS.2.68.*

CAMERON of DUNGALLON, ALEXANDER, Dungallon, Argyllshire, Major, Lochiel's, surrendered to General Campbell 6 March 1746. He was sent on parole to Inveraray; 6.3.1756/7 Edinburgh Castle, Edinburgh Jail, released 11 October 1749. "Was a standard bearer in the rebel army." After his surrender he was sent on parole to Inveraray. In March 1747 he went to Edinburgh and was committed to the Castle by the Lord Justice Clerk; he was still in jail, February 1749, having been excepted from the Act of Pardon of June 1747. In August he appealed for release under the Act of 1701 regarding wrongous imprisonment, and was discharged. When the Prince heard Dungallon had surrendered he said: "Why! I always looked upon Dungallon as a man of sense." *SHS.1.294, SHS.2.68.*

CAMERON of GLENEVIS, ALEXANDER, surrendered on 6.3.1746 to General Campbell, and sent on parole to Inveraray; 6.3.1746/7 Edinburgh Castle, released 7.7.1747. Alexander Cameron took no part in the Rising, but was imprisoned on suspicion of befriending relatives who were concerned. All his effects were plundered, his houses burnt, his wife and family grossly ill treated by the infamous Captain Carolina Scott, with a party of Government troops from Fort William. He surrendered to General Campbell and was sent to Inveraray on parole. In March 1747 he went to Edinburgh and was sent to the Castle by the Lord Justice Clerk. He was released under the Indemnity in July 1747. *SHS.2.68.*

CAMERON, ALEXANDER, aged 16, labourer from Lochaber, Inverness-shire, Lochiel's Regiment, imprisoned 6.11.1745 near Pentland Hills; 15.11746 Edinburgh Castle; Edinburgh Jail; 8.8.1746 Carlisle; Chester Castle. He was apparently deserting when he was captured. Transported to Antigua 8.5.1747. *SHS.2.70, MR30.*

CAMERON, ALEXANDER, aged 20, labourer from Lochaber, Inverness-shire, Lochiel's Regiment, imprisoned 6.11.1745 near Pentland Hills; Edinburgh Castle, 15.1.1746 Edinburgh Jail. He was apparently trying to desert when captured. Released under General Pardon, 1747. *SHS.2.70.*

CAMERON, ALEXANDER, from Appin, Argyll, Lochiel's Regiment, 22.9.1745 shot through back and chest at Prestonpans. He was taken prisoner when the Prince's army left Edinburgh. In Royal Infirmary, Edinburgh, 25.6.1746 Edinburgh Jail, died 18.10.1746. *SHS.1.186, SHS.2.70.*

CAMERON, ALEXANDER, aged 19, labourer from Lochaber, Inverness-shire, Lochiel's Regiment, taken at capture of Carlisle 30.12.1745, and also imprisoned in York Castle. Transported 31.3.1747. *SHS.2.70, MR33.*

CAMERON, ALEXANDER, (5) from Lochaber, Inverness-shire, Lochiel's Regiment, taken prisoner 30.12.1745 capture of Carlisle, also imprisoned in York Castle. There is no further reference to his disposal. *SHS.2.70.*

CAMERON, ALEXANDER, aged 19, from Inverness, McIntosh's Regiment, imprisoned Inverness and Tilbury Fort. "Maker of carts at Lord Murray's Dunmaglass." Transported 31.3.1747, or 5.5.1747 from Liverpool to Leeward Islands in *Veteran*, arriving Martinique June 1747. *SHS.2.70, MR33, PRO.SP36.102, MR174.*

CAMERON, ALEXANDER, from Torbane, Sunart, Argyll-shire, imprisoned Edinburgh, released under General Pardon, 1747. "Confesses that he joined the rebels but was forced thereto." *SHS.2.72.*

CAMERON, ALEXANDER, aged 25, farmer in Glenurquhart, Inverness-shire, Glengarry's Regiment, imprisoned Inverness, prison ship *Dolphin* Aug 1746, Tilbury Fort. He was not transported with the others, and probably died. *SHS.2.72.*

CAMERON of CALLART, ALLAN, aged 40, from Inverness, Captain, Locheil's Regiment and Artillery, imprisoned Culloden, Inverness June 1746, prison ship *Thane of Fife*, Tilbury Nov 1746, London (Southwark), sentenced to death but reprieved and banished 1748. "Principal servant to Locheil." He was wounded at Culloden, having an arm broken. He was brutally treated on board ship on the journey to London. He was tried in London in November 1746. In the evidence at his trial it transpired that he had saved one of the English officers from being killed. Nevertheless he was sentenced to death, but was pardoned on condition of leaving the country and never returning. *SHS.2.72.*

CAMERON, ANGUS, from Burnfoord, Lochaber, Inverness-shire, Duke of Perth's Regiment, imprisoned Canongate 8.8.1746, Carlisle. Further history not traced. *SHS.2.72.*

CAMERON, ANNE (and her female child aged 2 months), aged 28 (or 18), from Lochaber, Inverness-shire, "knits and spins", imprisoned 30.12.1745 Carlisle and Lancaster Castle. Transported to Antigua 8.5.1747, or from Liverpool to Leeward Islands in *Veteran*, arriving Martinique June 1747. *SHS.2.72, PRO.SP36.102.*

CAMERON, ARCHIBALD, Dr, brother of Cameron of Lochiel, Inverness, was one of the first to meet the Prince on his landing, though he was in the unpleasant position of being th bearer of a message to him from that Chief urging him to return to France. During the campaign he was employed as a combatant officer; and in this capacity his first exploit was the unsuccessful attempt on 28 August 1745 to capture the barracks at Ruthven. After Culloden he was in concealment for some months and succeeded in escapting to France with the Prince. He returned home in 1753, thinking he was safe in doing so, but was captured at the house of Stewart of Glenbucket and imprisoned in Edinburgh Castle, Tyburn and the Tower of London. He had no trial, but was sentenced to death and executed at Tyburn, 7 June 1753, the principal charge against him being that he was in possession of blank commissions signed by the Prince. A monument to him, the last victim of the '45, was put up to his memory in the Chapel vault of the old Savoy Chapel, where he is buried. Sanford Terry says the reason for his execution was "his implication in the hare-brained Elibank plot, serious only because of Frederick the Great's suspected connivance." *SHS.2.72.*

CAMERON, ARCHIBALD, from Sunart, Argyll, Tacksman of Auchenellan. "An officer in Lochiel's Regiment for some time and surrendered at Strontian to the Argyleshire levies, as a private man, 9 June 1746 but on discovery that he was an officer he was taken up by order of General Campbell. Imprisoned, 14.6.1746 Dumbarton Castle, discharged 18.7.1747. *SHS.2.74.*

CAMERON, DANIEL or DONALD, aged 40, from Ardnamurchan, Argyllshire, Lochiel's Regiment. Wounded in the leg at the battle of Prestonpans and taken prisoner when the Prince left Edinburgh, and sent to Carlisle. Imprisoned 21.9.1745 Prestonpans, 22.9.1745 Edinburgh Royal Infirmary, Edinburgh Tolbooth 8.8.1746, Carlisle, York Castle. Transported 31.3.1747. *SHS.2.74, MR34.*

CAMERON, DONALD, aged 30, farmer from Glenurquhart, Inverness-shire, Glengarry's Regiment, imprisoned Inverness and Tilbury Fort. Transported 31.3.1747. *SHS.2.74, MR150, BMHS.30.75.*

CAMERON, DONALD, aged 48, farmer near Fort William, Inverness-shire, Lochiel's Regiment, imprisoned in Inverness June 1746, prison ship *Margaret & Mary* June 1746, and prison ship *James & Mary*, Medway. Transported 31.3.1747 to Barbados in *Frere. SHS.2.76, MR34, PRO.CO137.58, BMHS.30.75.*

CAMERON, DONALD, aged 20, chapman at Rahoy in Morven, Argyllshire, Lochiel's Regiment, imprisoned in Inverness June 1746, prison ship *Dolphin* Sept 1746, prison ship *Pamela*, Tilbury. Transported 31.3.1747 in St *George or*

Carteret, arrived Jamaica 1747. *SHS.2.76, MR34, PRO.CO137.58.*

CAMERON, DONALD, from Gortanorn, Ardnamurchan, Argyllshire, Lochiel's Regiment, imprisoned July 1747 Ardnamurchan, 4.2.1747 Glasgow, Edinburgh, liberated 9.4.1747. Was in hospital with "the bones of his leg fractured in different places." *SHS.2.76.*

CAMERON, DONALD, aged 70, from Argyll, Lochiel's Regiment, imprisoned in Inverness June 1746, prison ship *Alexander & James* Tilbury, Tilbury Fort. No further reference to him. He probably died. *SHS.2.76.*

CAMERON, DONALD, from Tarbert, Ardnamurchan, Argyllshire, Lochiel's Regiment, Imprisoned July 1746 Ardnamurchan, 4.2.1747 Glasgow, liberated 15.7.1747. *SHS.2.76.*

CAMERON, DONALD, younger of Lochiel, escaped to France, died in 1748. *SHS.1.294.*

CAMERON *alias* McOLLONIE, DOUGAL, from Tarbert, Ardnamurchan, Argyllshire, Lochiel's Regiment, imprisoned July 1746 Ardnamurchan, 4.2.1747 Glasgow, discharged 15.7.1747. *SHS.2.76.*

CAMERON, DOUGAL, from Inverness, Lochiel's Regiment, taken at capture of Carlisle, imprisoned 30.12.1745 Carlisle, York Castle, Chester Castle. Transported 21.3.1747, or 24.2.1747 from Liverpool, in *Gildart*, arriving Port North Potomac, Maryland 1747. *SHS.2.76, MR34, PRO.T1.328.*

CAMERON, DUNCAN, from Island of Barra, "In charge of the Prince's baggage," imprisoned November 1745 Dalkeith, Edinburgh, released 19.6.1747. "Duncan Cameron says he was once a servant of old Lochiel at Boulogne, and had joined Lord John Drummond's regiment." While in Tournai he was asked by Aeneas Macdonald to go at once to Amiens and then to Nantes. Here he found he was wanted to accompany the Prince to Scotland, owing to his local knowledge of the Islands. He has left an account of the Prince" landing down to the time of the entry into Edinburgh. When the Prince set out for England, Cameron was in charge of the Prince's baggage. He was thrown from his horse and so severely damaged that he was left at a house near Dalkeith. It was reported that he was lying there, and it was imagined he was Colonel Strickland. He was sent to Edinburgh Tolbooth, where he was left. He says he escaped "either through sickness or want of evidence" when others were sent off to be tried in Carlisle. He was released some time before the Indemnity, but, instead of going home, went to Holland. Apparently no one ever knew he was one of the Prince's companions in the *Doutelle*. *SHS.2.78.*

CAMERON, DUNCAN, aged 70, from Moidart, imprisoned 16.1.1746 Cranston, Jan 1746 Edinburgh Jail, Canongate 8.8.1746 Carlisle. Servant to Aeneas Macdonald. Transported 21.3.1747 from London to Barbados in *Frere*. *SHS.2.78, MR9.*

CAMERON, DUNCAN, servant to Ranald Macdonald, younger of Clanranald. "Confesses that he took care of Clanranald's baggage during part of the rebellion." Imprisoned Edinburgh, released under General Pardon, 1747. *SHS.2.78.*

CAMERON, DUNCAN, from Glenmoriston, Inverness-shire, Glengarry's Regiment, imprisoned Edinburgh and released under General pardon, 1747. "Says he came to Edinburgh while the rebels were there as servant to one James Grant. Denies that he was in arms with them." *SHS.2.78.*

CAMERON, DUNCAN, labourer from Strathspey, Glengarry's Regiment, imprisoned 4.11.1745 Duddingston, 25.1.1746 Edinburgh Jail, released under General Pardon, 1747. He probably deserted from the Prince's army at Duddingston. *SHS.2.78.*

CAMERON, DUNCAN, aged 32, husbandman in Glenmoriston, Glenurquhart, Inverness-shire, Glengarry's Regiment, imprisoned May 1746 Inverness, prison ship *Dolphin,* Tilbury Fort Transported 31.3.1747 from Tilbury to Barbados in *Frere. SHS.2.78, MR150, BMHS.30.75.*

CAMERON, DUNCAN, "A common highlander" from Inverness, Glengarry's Regiment, imprisoned 4.11.1745 Duddingston, Edinburgh Castle, 15.1.1746 Edinburgh Jail, released under General Pardon, 1747. The place of his capture suggests that he deserted while the Prince's army was in camp at Duddingston. *SHS.2.78.*

CAMERON, EFFIE, aged 28, from Lochaber, Inverness-shire, imprisoned in Carlisle and Lancaster Castle. Captured at fall of Carlisle, "knits and spins." Transported 8.5.1747 to Antigua, or from Liverpool to Leeward Islands in *Veteran*, arriving Martinique 1747. *SHS.2.80, PRO.SP.36.102.*

CAMERON, EWEN, aged 30, husbandman in Hillhouses, Ross-shire, Lord Lovat's Regiment, imprisoned Inverness, *James & Mary*, Medway, Tilbury. Transported 19.3.1747 from

Tilbury to Jamaica in *St George or Carteret*, arriving Jamaica 1747. *SHS.2.80, MR117, PRO.CO.137.58, BMHS.30.75.*

CAMERON, EWEN, from Lochaber, Inverness-shire, Lochiel's Regiment, imprisoned March 1746 Fort William, Edinburgh. Uncle of Allan Cameron of Callart. He was wounded at the siege of Fort William in March 1746 and taken prisoner, and sent to Edinburgh. It has been suggested that he is identical with Hugh Cameron, who was executed at Carlisle on 18 October 1746, but this cannot be, as the siege of Fort William lasted until 4 April and Hugh Cameron was taken prisoner on 1 February 1746 at Montrose. He was probably released at the Indemnity. *SHS.2.80.*

CAMERON, EWEN MORE, aged 52, ale seller in Maryburgh near Fort William, Inverness-shire, Lochiel's Regiment. Imprisoned Inverness Sept 1746, prison ship *Pamela* Tilbury. Transported 19.3.1747 from Tilbury to Jamaica, in *St George & Carteret*, arriving Jamaica 1747. *SHS.2.80, MR34, PRO.CO137.58.*

CAMERON, FLORA, (and her child), aged 40, from Lochaber, Inverness-shire, captured at the fall of Carlisle, imprisoned Carlisle and Lancaster Castle. Transported to Antigua 8.5.1747, or from Liverpool to Leeward Islands in *Veteran*, arriving Martinique June 1747 *SHS.2.80, PRO.SP36.102.*

CAMERON, HUGH, of Annock (?Erracht), Captain, Lochiel's Regiment, imprisoned December 1946 Fort William, January 1747 Inverness. "In December 1746 Hugh Cameron 6ft 7ins high.... was taken in a hut near to a great wood about 5 miles from Fort William, by a Lieutenant and party from that garrison.... He had by him a brace of pistols, a firelock, and a broad sword, but was deprived of the use of them by the soldiers who hauled him out of bed naked. About the beginning of January he was carried to Inverness fettered, and tied to two soldiers." His further disposal has not been traced. *SHS.2.80.*

CAMERON, HUGH, labourer from Lochaber, Inverness-shire, Lochiel's Regiment, imprisoned 6.11.1745 near Pentland Hills, 15.1.1746 Edinburgh Castle, Edinburgh Jail, released under General Pardon, 1747. "Says that a brother of Lochiel forced him to join." He must have been deserting, along with other Camerons, when captured. *SHS.2.80.*

CAMERON, HUGH, from Loch Arkaig, Lochaber, Inverness-shire, "A rebell officer," Lochiel's Regiment, imprisoned 1.2.1746 Montrose, 10.3.1746 Stirling Castle, Canongate 8.8.1746,

Carlisle, executed Carlisle 18.10.1746. The Stirling return shows that he had been "shot through thigh," and that the surgeon's fee was 6s8d. He was tried at Carlisle on 19 September 1746 and sentenced to death. *SHS.2.82.*

CAMERON, JEAN, Miss, of Glendessary, Inverness-shire, imprisoned Elphinstone 11.2.1746, Edinburgh Castle, discharged on bail 8.7.1746, released on bail 15.11.1746. On suspicion. Miss Jean or Jenny Cameron is said to have been daughter of Hugh Cameron of Glendessary, and to have joined the Prince when he set up his standard with 200 men whome she personally led at Prestonpans and Falkirk. On the other hand Aeneas Macdonald, in his account of the early days, says, "She was so far from accompanying the Prince's army that she went off with the rest of the spectators as soon as the army marched. Neither was she ever with the Prince," except when he had his court at Edinburgh. *SHS.2.82.*

CAMERON, JOHN, aged 22, weaver in Aigus, Ross-shire, Lord Lovat's Regiment, imprisoned Inverness June 1746, prison ship *Margaret & Mary,* and *James & Mary,* Tilbury. Transported 31.3.1747 from Tilbury to Barbados in *Frere. SHS.2.82, MR117, BMHS.30.75.*

CAMERON, JOHN, aged 60, labourer from Lochaber, Inverness-shire, Lochiel's Regiment, imprisoned 30.12.1745 Carlisle, York Castle. Taken at capture of Carlisle. Transported 31.3.1747 to Jamaica in *St George or Carteret,* arriving Jamaica 1747. *SHS.2.82, MR35, PRO.CO.137.58.*

CAMERON, JOHN, aged 70, labourer from Lochaber, Inverness-shire, Lochiel's Regiment, taken at capture of Carlisle, imprisoned Carlisle 30.12.1745, Lancaster Castle. Transported 31.3.1747 from London to Barbados in *Frere. SHS.2.82, MR35.*

CAMERON, JOHN, from Argyll, Lochiel's Regiment, imprisoned 22.9.1745 Edinburgh Royal Infirmary, 5.5.1746 Canongate, 8.8.1746 Carlisle, York Castle. At the battle of Prestonpans he was wounded with a fractured thigh, gunshot. "Wants the right legg." He was taken prisoner when the Prince's army left Edinburgh. As there is no evidence of his transportation, he probably died in prison. *SHS.2.82.*

CAMERON, JOHN, aged 33, labourer from Lochaber, Inverness-shire, Lochiel's Regiment, imprisoned 6.11.1745 near Pentland Hills, 15.1.1746 Edinburgh Castle, Edinburgh Jail, Canongate, 8.8.1746 Carlisle. "He was evidently trying to desert when caught." Transported 31.3.1747. *SHS.2.84, MR35.*

CAMERON, JOHN, from Strontian, imprisoned Edinburgh Tolbooth, released under General Pardon, 1747. "A whiskie maker in Strontian. Confesses that he marched with the rebels to Lauder and made his escape from there. Denies he carried arms." *SHS.2.84.*

CAMERON, KENNETH, aged 21, husbandman in Lochmallin, Ross-shire, Lord Cromarty's Regiment, imprisoned Inverness, prison ship *Thane of Fife*, and *Liberty & Property*, Medway. Transported 31.3.1747 to Jamaica, in *St George or Carteret*, arriving Jamaica 1747. Mons. Carpentier tried to claim him as a French soldier of the French Royal Scots, but did not succeed. *SHS.2.84, PRO.C.137.58, BMHS.30.75.*

CAMERON, MALCOLM, from Fort William, Inverness-shire, Lochiel's Regiment, imprisoned 21.9.1745 Prestonpans, 22.9.1745 Edinburgh Royal Infirmary, 5.5.1746 Canongate, 8.8.1746 Carlisle, transported 21.3.1747,or 24.2.1747 from Liverpool in *Gildart*, arriving Port North Potomac, Maryland, 5 Aug 1747. Shot through the ankle at the battle of Prestonpans and taken prisoner after the departure of the Prince's army. He was probably the "Malckarn" Cameron whose name appears in the Carlisle transportation lists. *SHS.2.84, MR35, PRO.T1.328.*

CAMERON, MURDOCH, aged 31 from Inverness, Lochiel's Regiment, imprisoned Inverness June 1746, prison ship *Alexander & James* Tilbury, released. There is no further reference to his disposal. *SHS.2.86.*

CAMERON, PETER, Vintner from Edinburgh, imprisoned on suspicion 6.2.1747 Edinburgh Castle, released June 1747. *SHS.2.86.*

CAMERON, WILLIAM, aged 35, farmer in Glenurquhart, Inverness-shire, Glengarry's Regiment, imprisoned Inverness June 1746, prison ship *Dolphin* Tilbury Fort, transported 31.3.1747 from Tilbury to Barbados in *Frere*. *SHS.2.86, PRO.SP36.102, BMHS.30.75.*

CAMERON, WILLIAM, aged 50, farmer in Glenmoriston, Inverness-shire, Glengarry's Regiment, imprisoned Inverness June 1746, prison ship *Dolphin* Tilbury. Transported 31.3.1747 from Tilbury. *SHS.2.88, BMHS.30.75.*

CAMPBELL, AENEAS or ANGUS, "A common highlander in the rebel service," from Lochaber, Inverness-shire, imprisoned

4.11.1745 Dalkeith, Edinburgh Castle, 15.1.1746 Edinburgh, Carlisle, York Castle, transported 4.9.1748. From the date of his capture he must have been one of the stragglers or deserters on the march south. *SHS.2.88.*
CAMPBELL, ALEXANDER, aged 30, drover from Lochaber, Inverness-shire, Lochiel's Regiment, imprisoned 30.12.1745 Carlisle, Lincoln Castle, transported 22.4.1747. Taken at capture of Carlisle. This may have been the man who appealed for release in February 1751 and said he had been ill, and was overlooked for transportation. *SHS.2.88.*
CAMPBELL, ALEXANDER, aged 40, from Argyll, imprisoned Carlisle, York Castle, transported to Antigua 8.5.1747 from Liverpool to Leeward Islands in *Veteran*, arriving Martinique June 1747. *SHS.2.88, PRO.SP36.102.*
CAMPBELL, DANIEL, aged 20. *BMHS.30.75.*
CAMPBELL, DONALD, aged 21, husbandman from Lentiarm, Ross-shire, Lord Cromarty's Regiment, imprisoned Inverness, prison ship *Thane of Fife* June 1746, prison ship *Liberty & Property* Medway, transported 31.3.1747 from Tilbury to Jamaica in *St George & Carteret*, arriving Jamaica 1747. *SHS.2.90, PRO.CO.137.58, BMHS.30.75.*
CAMPBELL, DONALD, aged 25 from Ross-shire, Lord Cromarty's Regiment, imprisoned Inverness, prison ship *Thane of Fife* June 1746, prison ship *Liberty & Property* Tilbury. Transported 31.3.1747 from Tilbury to Jamaica in *St George or Carteret*, arriving Jamaica 1747 *SHS.2.90, MR81, PRO.CO.137.58, BMHS.30.75.*
CAMPBELL, DOUGALL, aged 18, servant from Lochaber, Inverness-shire, imprisoned Whitehaven, Carlisle, York Castle. Transported Antigua 8.5.1747, or from Liverpool to Leeward Islands in *Veteran*, arriving Martinique June 1747. *SHS.2.90, PRO.SP.36.102.*
CAMPBELL, DUNCAN, aged 24 from Ross-shire, Cromarty's Regiment, imprisoned Inverness June 1746, prison ship *Jane of Leith*, Tilbury. Transported 20.3.1747 from Tilbury to Jamaica in *St George or Carteret*, arriving Jamaica 1747. *SHS.2.90, MR81, PRO.CO.137.58.*
CAMPBELL, DUNCAN, aged 16, labourer from Argyll, imprisoned Carlisle, York Castle, Lincoln Castle. Transported Antigua 8.5.1747, or from Liverpool to Leeward Islands in *Veteran*, arriving Martinique June 1747. *SHS.2.92, PRO.SP.36.102.*
CAMPBELL, DUNCAN, aged 17, from Island of South Uist, Lord George Murray's Regiment, imprisoned in Inverness, prison

ship *HMS Furnace* June 1746, prison ship *Liberty & Property*, Tilbury. Released 10.6.1747. Apprentice tailor in Breadalbane; against his name is stated that he was "Evidence against Clanranald and others." This was probably the man who was in the custody of Dick, the messenger, in June 1747, and was released. *SHS.2.92.*

CAMPBELL, EWEN (EVANDER), aged 20, from Ross-shire, imprisoned Inverness June 1746, prison ship *Jane of Leith*, Aug 1746, prison ship *Liberty & Property*, Tilbury. Transported 31.3.1747 from Tilbury to Jamaica or Barbados. *SHS.2.902, MR81, BMHS.30.75.*

CAMPBELL, GILBERT, aged 18, servant to Janet Gordon, from Sutherland, imprisoned on suspicion Inverness June 1746, prison ship *Wallsgrave*, Tilbury Fort. Transported 31.3.1747 from Tilbury to Barbados in *Frere SHS.2.92, MR127, BMHS.30.75.*

CAMPBELL, HECTOR, aged 20, farmer from Caithness, Lord Cromarty's Regiment, imprisoned 15.4.1746 Sutherland, inverness June 1746, prison ship *Wallsgrave*, Tilbury Fort. Discharged. He gave evidence against prisoners at the Southwark trials. *SHS.2.92*

CAMPBELL, Sir JAMES of Auchinbreck, Argyll, imprisoned 21.11.1745 Auchinbreck, 25.11.1745 Dumbarton Castle. MP for Argyllshire in the Scottish Parliament 1702-07. He was father-in-law of Donald Cameron of Lochiel. He died in 1756. His wife was daughter of John Macleod of Macleod and aunt of Norman Macleod, the chief in 1745. When apprehended letters were found upon him from Dugald McTavish of Dunardary directed to him, and of a "treasonable" nature. He was specially excepted from the Act of pardon of June 1747. *SHS.2.94*

CAMPBELL, JAMES, a boy, from Thurso, Caithness, imprisoned in Edinburgh, released under General Pardon, 1747. Says he never joined the rebel army. *SHS.2.94*

CAMPBELL, JOHN, from Inverness, Glengarry's Regiment, imprisoned 30.12.1745 Carlisle. Transported Antigua 8.5.1747. Taken at capture of Carlisle, pleaded guilty when brought to trial, sentenced to death. *SHS.2.94*

CAMPBELL, JOHN, aged 15, servant from Rannoch, Argyllshire, imprisoned 24.2.1746 Perth, August 1746 Edinburgh, Canongate, August 1746 Carlisle, Lancaster Castle. Transported Antigua 8.5.1747, or from Liverpool to Leeward Islands in *Veteran*, arriving Martinique June 1747. The

transportation list describes him as a "sprightly lad."
SHS.2.96, MR151, PRO.SP36.102.
CAMPBELL, JOHN, fisherman from Island of Mull, imprisoned 19.3.1746 Stirling, Carlisle, transported 21.3.1747. In the rebellion. "Says that he came to Crieff with the rebels and deserted there." *SHS.2.96.*
CAMPBELL, JOHN, aged 14, "A common highlander soldier's son" from Caithness, imprisoned 4.11.1745 Duddingston, 15.1.1746 Edinburgh Tolbooth, discharged 18.6.1747. *SHS.2.88.*
CAMPBELL, JOHN, from Argyllshire, Cromarty's Regiment, imprisoned in Inverness, prison ship *Wallsgrave*, Tilbury. Died on prison ship *Wallsgrave* 12 June 1746. *SHS.2.96, SHS.1.186.*
CAMPBELL, JOHN, aged 21, blacksmith in Skerhiese, Ross-shire, Cromarty's Regiment, imprisoned Inverness, prison ship *Liberty*, Medway. Transported 21.9.1748. *SHS.2.96.*
CAMPBELL, PETER, from Ballintombuy, Glenmoriston, Inverness-shire, Glengarry's Regiment, imprisoned Inverness. "Influenced by his superior to rise in arms." Nothing more is known about him. *SHS.2.98.*
CAMPBELL, WILLIAM, aged 18, tailor, parish of Rea, Caithness, Lord Cromarty's Regiment, imprisoned Inverness June 1746, prison ship *Thane of Fife*, and prison ship *James & Mary*, Tilbury. Transported 31.3.1747 from Tilbury to Jamaica in *St George or Carteret*, arriving Jamaica 1747. *SHS.2.98, MR81, PRO.CO137.58, BMHS.30.75.*
CARROLL, ALEXANDER, aged 27, labourer from Argyllshire, imprisoned Carlisle and Lancaster Castle. Nothing more is known of him. *SHS.2.102.*
CATTANACH, ALEXANDER, aged 17, miller from Badenoch, Inverness-shire, imprisoned in Carlisle, York. Transported Antigua 8.5.1747, or from Liverpoolto Leeward Islands in *Veteran*, arriving Martinique June 1747. *SHS.2.104, PRO.SP36.102.*
CHISHOLM, DONALD, aged 23, from Inverness, Lord John Drummond's Regiment, imprisoned Inverness June 1746, prison ship *Alexander & James,* and prison ship *James & Mary*, Medway, Tilbury, discharged. "Enlisted at Inverness and sent to Dunkirk," presumably to join the troops of the French army being raised there. This was the man who gave evidence against Charles Oliphant. *SHS.2.112.*

CHISHOLM, DONALD, aged 26, from Blairy, Glenurquhart, Inverness-shire, Glengarry's Regiment. Imprisoned Inverness June 1746, prison ship *Dolphin* Tilbury. Transported 21.3.1747 from Tilbury to Jamaica in *St George or Carteret*, arriving Jamaica 1747. *SHS.2.112, MR151, PRO.CO.137.58.*

CHISHOLM, DONALD, aged 27, farmer in Glenmoriston, Inverness-shire, Glengarry's Regiment, imprisoned Inverness June 1746, prison ship *Wallsgrave*, Tilbury Fort, transported 21.3.1747. *SHS.2.112, MR151.*

CHISHOLM, JOHN, aged 40, weaver in Invercannich, Inverness-shire, Chisholm's Regiment, imprisoned in Inverness June 1746, prison ship *Liberty & Property*. Transported 31.3.1747 from London to Jamaica, in *St Geroge or Carteret*, arriving Jamaica 1747. *SHS.2.114, PRO.CO.137.58, BMHS.30.75.*

CHISHOLM, PERCY, aged 47, from Inverness, Chisholm's Regiment. Imprisoned Inverness June 1746, prison ship *Alexander & James*, Tilbury. He probably died, as he was not on the transportation lists. *SHS.2.114.*

CLANNISH, GEORGE, aged 60, from Ross-shire, Cromarty's Regiment, imprisoned Inverness June 1746, prison ship *Jane of Leith*, Tilbury. No further reference to him. *SHS.2.114.*

CLARK, HENRY, McIntosh's Regiment, died in Carlisle prison, November 1746. *SHS.1.186.*

CLARKE, DONALD, aged 38, from Argyllshire, Lord John Drummond's Regiment, imprisoned Inverness June 1746, prison ship *Alexander & James*, Tilbury. No further reference to him. *SHS.2.116.*

COLBERT, LANCELOT, aged 33, from Inverness, Colonel, Lord John Drummond's Regiment, imprisoned Inverness June 1746, prison ship *Alexander & James*, Marshalsea. Pardoned on condition of perpetual banishment. 3.7.1747 *SHS.2.120.*

COLQUHOUN, ARCHIBALD, aged 32, farmer in Appin, Argyll, Stewart of Ardshiel's Regiment, imprisoned Inverness June 1747, prison ship *Liberty & Property*, Tilbury. Transported 20.3.1747 from Tilbury ot Jamaica or Barbados in *St George or Carteret*, arrived Jamaica 1747. *SHS.2.122, MR14, PRO.CO137.58, BMHS.30.74.*

COLQUHOUN, ARCHIBALD, of Colhoun, McIntosh's Regiment, died at sea on prison ship *Alexander & James,* 6 May 1746. *SHS.1.186.*

COLQUHOUN, ROBERT, wright from Luss, Argyllshire, imprisoned on suspicion 8.9.1745 Dumbarton. Discharged 28.8.1746. *SHS.2.122.*

CROMARTIE, Earl of, GEORGE MACKENZIE, Imprisoned 15.4.1746 Dunrobin; Inverness 28.4.1746, HMS *Exeter* 20.5.1746, Tower of London, House of Cowell, messenger. Conditionally pardoned 4 Oct 1749. Though at first inclined to the Government side, Lord Cromartie ultimaely declared for the Prince and joined the Army at Perth. He was employed in collecting money in Fife, and was present at the battle of Falkirk on 17 Jan 1746. He took over command of Kilmarnock" Guards for a time. He was put in command of the operations against the Earl of Loudon, and pursued him for some time without success, and was superseded. On 15 April he was captured by the Sutherland Militia, sent to London, and committed to the Tower. On 28 July 1746 he was tried before the House of Lords, pleaded guilty and was sentenced to death, with forfeiture of estates and honours. He was respited on 9 August largely through the instrumentality of his wife and some of his friends who interceded for him. On 18 February 1748 he was allowed to leave the Tower and to live in the house of a messenger. On 4 October 1749 he had a pardon on condition of his confining himself during his life to such part of England as His Majesty shall, from time to time, direct. He died in London 28 Sept 1766 in an impoverished state. *SHS.2.136.*

CUMMING, DUNCAN, aged 65, from Auchtuie, Glenurquhart, Inverness-shire, glengarry's Regiment, imprisoned Inverness June 1746, prison ship *Dolphin.* Discharged 13.5.1746. "Went with the rebels the day before Culloden and never received arms nor pay." *SHS.2.140.*

CUMMING, JAMES, aged 36, son of Duncan Cumming from Pitcherell-Beg, Glenurquhart, Inverness-shire, Glengarry's Regiment. Imprisoned Inverness, prison ship *Dolphin,* Tilbury Fort. "Forced, but reckoned a plunderer in the North." Disposal is unknown, probably died. *SHS.2.140.*

CUMMING, JAMES, from Achnagoneren, Glenmoriston, Inverness-shire, Glengarry's Regiment (pressed), imprisoned in Inverness and Tilbury Fort. *SHS.2.140.*

CUMMINS, STEPHEN, Officer of Excise from Campbeltown, Argyll, imprisoned Lancaster Gate, released 30.11.1747. "Joined the rebels at Edinburgh, drank treasonable healths and spoke disrespectfully of HRH the Duke of Cumberland. Prisoner in Dumbarton Castle." *SHS.2.140.*

CUNNINGHAM, DUNCAN, servant boy from Argyllshire, imprisoned "on suspicion" 2.2.1746 Kilsyth, 7.2.1746 Stirling Castle, and Leith. Discharged. *SHS.2.140.*

CUNNINGHAM, JOHN, aged 30, labourer from Argyllshire, Duke of Perth's Regiment, imprisoned Carlisle, Lancaster Castle. Transported Antigua 8.5.1747, or from Liverpool to Leeward Islands in *Veteran,* arriving Martinique June 1747. *SHS.2.140, PRO.SP36.102, MR70.*

DARA, ROBERT, from Skye, imprisoned 7.2.1746, Stirling Castle, released under General Pardon, 1747. "In the rebellion." *SHS.2.144.*

DAVIDSON, ALEXANDER, aged 17, from Badenoch, imprisoned Stirling, Canongate, 8.8.1746 Carlisle, York Castle. Sentenced to be transported Antigua 8.5.1747 but pardoned on condition of enlistment. *SHS.2.144.*

DINGWALL, DONALD, aged 24, servant to Farquhar McCrae, from Ross-shire, Cromarty's Regiment, imprisoned Inverness, Tilbury Fort, transported 31.3.1747 from Tilbury to Barbados in *Frere. SHS.2.154, MR81, BMHS.30.75.*

DINGWALL, DUNCAN, aged 28, from Cromarty, Cromarty's Regiment, imprisoned Inverness, prison ship *Jane of Leith*, Tilbury. His name does not appear in the transportation lists, so he probably died. *SHS.2.154.*

DONALD, JAMES, aged 20, tailor from Caithness, Lord George Murray's Regiment, taken at the capture of Carlisle and imprisoned 30.12.1745 Carlisle, Lincoln Castle. Transported Antigua 8.5.1747. *SHS.2.156.*

DOW, WILLIAM, from Achtmeerak, Glenurquhart, Glengarry's Regiment, (forced), imprisoned 6.5.1746 Inverness. *SHS.2.162.*

DUNCAN, JOHN, aged 21, from Ross-shire, husbandman, Cornie, Banff, Lord John Drummond's Regiment. Imprisoned Culloden, Inverness, June 1746 prison ship *James & Mary*, Medway. He probably died as he is not in the transportation lists. *SHS.2.172.*

ELDER, WILLIAM, aged 18, from Ross-shire, servant to William McKenzie "a rebel captain" in Kilcoy. Cromarty's Regiment, imprisoned in Inverness, June 1746 prison ship *Alexander &*

James, prison ship *Liberty & Property* Tilbury. Transported 31.3.1747 from London to Barbados in *Frere. SHS.2.178, MR81, BMHS.30.75.*

FALCONER, CHARLES, Attorney from Inverness, imprisoned Inverness. Taken on suspicion. "Witnesses testify to treasonable speeches that, when His Majesty went abroad, he wished he might never return. Others heard him propose and drink to the Pretender's health and wish success to his cause." One Lachlan Dallas said he had heard him say while George II was abroad, that he "wished he might never return." He does not appear in any of the transports. He may have been discharged, or possibly he died at sea. *SHS.2.180.*

FARQUHARSON, ALEXANDER, aged 40, farmer from Achnriachan, Glenmoriston. Glengarry's Regiment, imprisoned in Inverness, prison ship *Dolphin*, Tilbury. Transported 31.3.1747 from London to Barbados in *Frere.* He was one of the very few who escaped from America and returned home. *SHS.2.182, MR.151, BMHS.30.75.*

FARQUHARSON, CHARLES, The Rev, from Braemar. Imprisoned Inverness, Tilbury, Southwark, in custody of Dick the messenger. Released on condition of departing the kingdom and not returning, May 1747. "Jesuit Priest. Was a witness to his brother, John, in Strathglass. He left Scotland in 1729, studied at Madrid and Douai, and in obedience to the order of his superior, Francisco Ritz, General of the Jesuits, delivered to him on 26 July last, he returned to Scotland and, being appointed to no certain place, he went to his brother, said John." *SHS.2.182.*

FARQUHARSON, DONALD, aged 32, from Achnagoren, Glenmoriston, Glengarry's Regiment. Imprisoned Inverness Oct 1746, Tilbury Fort. Transported 31.3.1747 from London to Barbados in *Frere.* He escaped from America with Alexander Farquharson and got home. *SHS.2.182, MR151.*

FARQUHARSON, DUNCAN, aged 23 from Glenmoriston, Farquharson's Regiment, imprisoned Inverness and Tilbury, transported 31.3.1747 from London to Barbados in *Frere*. *SHS.2.182, MR202, BMHS.30.76.*

FARQUHARSON, FRANCIS of Monaltrie, Farquharson's Regiment, imprisoned Culloden, Inverness June 1746, London, House of Munie, messenger. Released 1766. Commonly called the "Baron Ban" on account of his fair hair. Francis Farquharson of Monaltrie joined the Prince after

Prestonpans on 3 October 1745 with 30 men. He himself did not go to England but served in the actions of Inverury, Falkirk, and Culloden. At Culloden he was taken prisoner and sent to Inverness and thence to London, where he was tried and pleaded guilty; on 15 November sentenced to death. He was reprieved the day before the execution and sent to the house of Munie, messenger. He was soon afterwards pardoned on condition that he went and remained abroad but this condition was altered to one binding him to confine himself to such place in England as the King directed. Accordingly he was kept a partial prisoner in England at Berkhamstead until 1766, when he was released. In 1775 he asked to be allowed to rent some of his forfeited estates. This was granted. He died 1791. *SHS.2.182.*

FARQUHARSON, PETER, aged 40, from Achnagoren, Glenmoriston, Glengarry's Regiment, imprisoned in Inverness and Tilbury Fort. "Never in arms till forced in March last." Transported 31.3.1747 from London to Barbados in *Frere*. *SHS.2.186, MR151, BMHS.30.76.*

FERGUSON, ALEXANDER, aged 30 from Glenurquhart, Glengarry's Regiment. Farmer in Glenmoriston. Imprisoned Inverness, prison ship *Dolphin*, Tilbury Fort, transported. *SHS.2.186, MR151.*

FERGUSON, DONALD, from Gartmore, Isle of Skye, Sergeant, Duke of Perth's Regiment, imprisoned 16.4.1746 Culloden, Inverness, Sept 1746 prison ship *Pamela*, Tilbury. Servant to MacDonald of Tormore. Transported 1747 from Tilbury. Servant to McDonald of Gartmore. This may have been the Donald Ferguson who appealed against transportation. He gave evidence against James Stewart. *SHS.2.188, MR68, BMHS.30.76.*

FERGUSON, FINLAY, aged 78, from Inverness. Imprisoned Inverness, Tilbury Fort. Merchant in "Touchtarter". On suspicion. Having regard to his age and the fact that he does not appear in the transportation lists, he probably died. *SHS.2.188.*

FERGUSON, WILLIAM, aged 55, farmer in Glenmoriston, Inverness-shire, Glengarry's Regiment, imprisoned May 1746 Inverness, June 1746 prison ship *Dolphin*, Tilbury. Transported 1747 from Tilbury. *SHS.2.190.*

FINLAYSON or FINLAY, ALEXANDER, aged 30, servant to John McInivire, Lochcarron, Ross-shire. Cromarty's Regiment, imprisoned Inverness, Tilbury Fort. Transported 20.3.1747 from Tilbury. *SHS.2.192, MR81.*

FINLAYSON or FINLAY, JOHN, aged 24, from Isle of Skye, servant to Donald McLeod in Ballygower. Cromarty's Regiment, imprisoned Inverness, Tilbury Fort. Transported 20.3.1747. *SHS.2.192, MR81.*

FLINT, JAMES, from Inverness-shire, cadet in French Picquets, imprisoned 16.4.1746 Culloden Inverness. Discharged. *SHS.2.192.*

FORBES, ALEXANDER, aged 20 from Inverness-shire, imprisoned Inverness, June 1746 prison ship *Thane of Fife* Tilbury. "On suspicion." This may have been the man who is said to have "gone to the rebellion, a Servant to William Scott, late of Auchtydonald, on 1 Oct 1745." Not transported, may have died. *SHS.2.198.*

FORBES, ALEXANDER, aged 20, weaver in Beauly, Inverness, Lord Lovat's Regiment, imprisoned in Inverness, prison ship *Liberty & Property* Medway. Discharged. *SHS.2.200.*

FORBES, JAMES, Printer in Caithness. Roy Stuart's Regiment. Imprisoned 14.11.1745 West Port, Edinburgh; Edinburgh Castle, 16.1.1746 Edinburgh Jail, 8.8.1746 Carlisle. Pardoned on condition of enlistment. He pleaded guilty when brought to trial on 9 Sept 1746 and was sentenced to death. His execution was ordered for 21 Oct 1746, but he was reprieved. *SHS.2.200.*

FORBES, WILLIAM, aged 25, from Caithness, Cromarty's Regiment, imprisoned Inverness, prison ship *Thane of Fife* Tilbury. Not shown in the transportation lists. He probably died. *SHS.2.202.*

FRASER, ALEXANDER, aged 22, weaver from Monique, Inverness-shire, Lord Lovat's Regiment, imprisoned Inverness June 1746 prison ship *Alexander & James,* and prison ship *Liberty & Property* Tilbury. Transported 31.3.1747 from London to Barbados on *Frere.* *BMHS.30.76.*

FRASER, or FRIESEL, DANIEL, from Inverness, McDonald's Regiment, imprisoned Stirling, Carlisle, Coventry, York. Executed York 1.11.1746. Deserter from Loudoun's Regiment, tried 2 October 1746 at York and pleaded guilty. Was sentenced to death. "A very active Highlander." *SHS.2.208.*

FRASER, DAVID, aged 27, from Inverness. Sergeant, Lord Lovat's Regiment, imprisoned 16.4.1746 Culloden,

Inverness, June 1746 prison ship *Jane of Leith*, Tilbury, Tilbury Fort. Servant to the Master of Lovat. Transported 31.3.1747 from London to Barbados in *Frere*. *SHS.2.208, MR116, BMHS.30.76.*

FRASER, DAVID, aged 22, from Ross-shire, Cromarty's Regiment, imprisoned Inverness June 1746 prison ship *Jane of Leith*, Tilbury, Tilbury Fort. Fiddler of Ballachridhe. Transported 31.3.1747 from Tilbury. *SHS.22.210, MR81, BMHS.30.76.*

FRASER, DAVID, aged 22, from Balagalken, Glen Urquhart, Inverness-shire, Lord Lovat's Regiment, imprisoned on prison ship *Jane of Leith* Tilbury. "He is deaf and dumb but said to kill 7 men at Falkirk." Transported 20.3.1747 from London to Barbados on *Frere*. *SHS.2.210, MR117.*

FRASER, DONALD, aged 19, tailor from Logie, Ross-shire, Lord Cromarty's Regiment, imprisoned Inverness, prison ship *Thane of Fife*, and prison ship *Liberty & Property*, Tilbury. In spite of giving evidence against Lord Macleod he was apparently transported 31.3.1747 from London to Jamaica in *St George or Carteret*, arriving Jamaica 1747. *SHS.2.210, MR81, PRO.CO137.58, BMHS.30.76.*

FRASER, DONALD, aged 20, husbandman from Fort Augustus, Inverness-shire, Lord Lovat's Regiment, imprisoned 10.4.1746 Culloden, Inverness, June 1746 prison ship *Alexander & James,* and prison ship *Liberty,* Medway. Transported 20.3.1747 from London to Jamaica in *St George or Carteret*, arriving Jamaica 1747. *SHS.2.210, MR117, PRO.CO137.58, BMHS.30.76.*

FRASER, alias GARDINER, DONALD, aged 58, farmer in Achtemerak, Glen Urquhart, Inverness-shire. Glengarry's Regiment, imprisoned Inverness, June 1746 prison ship *Dolphin*, Tilbury Fort, discharged. He was probably the man who turned King's Evidence at the Southwark trials. *SHS.2.210.*

FRASER, HUGH, yr of Bochrubin, from Dunballoch, Inverness-shire. Imprisoned 1.7.1746 Fort Augustus, Inverness, Edinburgh Castle, London, House of Munie, messenger. Pardoned 7.6.1748. He is styled "Secretary to Lord Lovat." He was at the time a Writer in Edinburgh, but had been Secretary to Lord Lovat from 1741 until 1744, when he left him and was succeeded by Robert Fraser. The Duke of Newcastle had him sent to London. Murray of Broughton said Fraser had been sent to Lord Lovat to urge him to join the Prince. He was certainly carrying letters to Lovat in

January 1746. He turned King's Evidence against Lord Lovat. He, along with John Murray of Broughton, was granted a free pardon, the relevant letter being dated 7 June 1748. *SHS.2.210.*

FRASER, HUGH, aged 27, husbandman from Auchindach, Inverness. Lord John Drummond's Regiment, imprisoned Inverness June 1746, prison ship *Margaret & Mary*, Tilbury, and prison ship *Liberty & Property*. Transported 31.3.1747 from London to Jamaica in *St George or Carteret*, arriving Jamaica 1747. *SHS.2.212, MR62, PRO.CO137.58, BMHS.30.76.*

FRASER, HUGH or EWEN, aged 32 (80?), tailor in Colwoolen, Inverness, Lord Lovat's Regiment. Imprisoned Inverness, June 1746 prison ship *Alexander & James*, Tilbury, Tilbury Fort. Transported 31.3.1747 from London to Barbados on *Frere*. *SHS.2.212, MR117, BMHS.30.76.*

FRASER, HUGH, aged 26, husbandman in Imirmurie, Inverness, Lord Lovat's Regiment. Imprisoned Inverness, June 1746 prison ship *Margaret & Mary*, Tilbury. Transported 31.3.1747 from London to Jamaica in *St George or Carteret*, arriving Jamaica 1747. *SHS.2.212, MR117, PRO.CO137.28, BMHS.30.76.*

FRASER, HUGH, aged 26, husbandman in Drumhardinich, Inverness, Lord Lovat's Regiment. Imprisoned Inverness, June 1746 prison ship *Alexander & James*, and prison ship *Liberty*. Transported 31.3.1747 from London to Jamaica in *St George or Carteret*, arriving Jamaica 1747. *SHS.2.212, MR117, PRO.CO137.58, BMHS.30.76.*

FRASER, JAMES, aged 68, labourer from Inverness, Lord Lovat's Regiment. Imprisoned "on suspicion" Inverness, prison ship *Wallsgrave*, Tilbury, Tilbury Fort. Transported 31.3.1747 from London to Barbados in *Frere*. *SHS.2.212, MR118.*

FRASER, JOHN, Provost of Inverness, imprisoned Inverness and released. When he went in his official capacity to pay his respects to Cumberland after the battle of Culloden he asked that mercy be mingled with judgment. He was literally kicked out of the room by General Hawley's (or Huske's) orders with the words, "damn the rebel dog, kick him downstairs and throw him in prison directly." He was presumably released later, as he does not appear to have been sent to London. *SHS.2.214.*

FRASER, JOHN, aged 22, Delcaitack, Glenmoriston, Inverness-shire, Glengarry's Regiment. Imprisoned Inverness, prison ship *Wallsgrave*, Tilbury, Tilbury Fort. Transported 31.3.1747 from London to Barbados in *Frere*. "Farms some land near Culloden. Taken on suspicion he says." This may be the man who is shown as Captain O'Neill's servant in the Tilbury Lists. *SHS.2.214, MR151, BMHS.30.76.*

FRASER, JOHN, aged 40, from Inverwick, Glenmoriston, Inverness-shire, Glengarry's Regiment. Imprisoned Inverness, prison ship *Wallsgrave*, Tilbury. Transported 20.3.1747 to Barbados in *Frere*. *SHS.2.214, MR152.*

FRASER, JOHN, aged 50 (60?), farmer in Craigscory, Inverness, Lord Lovat's Regiment. Imprisoned Inverness, June 1746 prison ship *Alexander & James*, Tilbury, Tilbury Fort. Transported 31.3.1747 from London to Barbados in *Frere*. *SHS.2.214, MR118, BMHS.30.76.*

FRASER, JOHN, aged 34, weaver from Inverness, Lord Lovat's Regiment. Imprisoned Inverness, Tilbury Fort. Transported 31.3.1747 from London to Barbados in *Frere*. *SHS.2.214, MR118, BMHS.30.76.*

FRASER, JOHN, aged 22, from Inverness, Lord Lovat's Regiment. Imprisoned Inverness, Tilbury Fort, prison ship *Liberty & Property* Medway. Transported 31.3.1747. Servant to Mr Mitchell, Writer, Edinburgh. During the operations he was servant to O'Neill a French Officer." *SHS.2.214.*

FRASER, JOHN, aged 30, farmer in Crochill, Ross-shire, Lord Lovat's Regiment. Imprisoned Inverness, June 1746 prison ship *James & Mary* Medway. Transported 31.3.1747 from London to Barbados in *Frere SHS2.214, MR118, BMHS.30.76.*

FRASER, JOHN, aged 44, farmer in Belladrum, Inverness, Lord Lovat's Regiment. Imprisoned Inverness, prison ship *Liberty & Property* Medway. No further record. Probably died. *SHS.2.214.*

FRASER, JOHN, aged 30 from Inverness. Imprisoned "on suspicion" prison ship *Margaret & Mary* Tilbury. No further record. Probably died. *SHS.2.216.*

FRASER, OWEN, from Inverness. Imprisoned Inverness, Tilbury. Transported 20.3.1747 from Tilbury. *SHS.2.216.*

FRASER, PATRICK, aged 36, husbandman in Drumhardinich, Inverness-shire, Lord Lovat's Regiment. Imprisoned Inverness, prison ship *Liberty & Property* Medway. *SHS.2.216.*

FRASER, ROBERT, aged 22, Secretary to Lord Lovat, imprisoned Aug 1746 prison ship *Pamela* Tilbury. He became

Secretary to Lord Lovat after 1744, and is styled so when a prisoner. It was not he who gave evidence against Lord Lovat, though he said he was present at the meeting between the Prince and Lovat at Gortuleg after Culloden when Lovat excused himself for his not having taken part in the operations owing to his age and infirmities. His disposal has not been traced. *SHS.2.216.*

FRASER, RORY or RODERICK, aged 28, farmer from Dingwall, Ross-shire, Cromarty's Regiment. Imprisoned Inverness, prison ship *Wallsgrave*, Tilbury, Tilbury Fort. Transported 31.3.1747 from London to Barbados in *Frere*. *SHS.2.216, MR81, BMHS.30.76.*

FRASER, SIMON, aged 20, from Inverness, lived with his father in Aird, Lord Lovat's Regiment. Imprisoned Inverness, June 1746 prison ship *Jane of Leith*, Tilbury, Tilbury Fort. Transported 31.3.1747 from London to Jamaica in *St George or Carteret*, arrived Jamaica 1747. *SHS.2.216, MR118, PRO.CO137.58, BMHS.30.76.*

FRASER, WILLIAM, aged 26, from Aird, Inverness-shire. Husbandman in Kirktown. Lord Lovat's Regiment, imprisoned June 1746 prison ship *Margaret & Mary* Tilbury, and prison ship *James & Mary*. Transported 31.3.1747 from London to Jamaica in *St George or Carteret*, arriving Jamaica 1747. "Was apprehended after the battle of Falkirk." *SHS.2.218, MR118, PRO.CO137.58, BMHS.30.76.*

FRASER, WILLIAM, from Inverness, Lochiel's Regiment, imprisoned 20.11.1745 Leith; 25.11.1745 Edinburgh Jail, liberated 10.3.1746. "A common Highlander." *SHS.2.218.*

GARVE, WILLIAM, from Inchrory, Ross-shire, Cromarty's Regiment, imprisoned Inverness; Sept 1746 prison ship *Pamela* Tilbury. Transported 20.3.1747 from London to Barbados in *Frere*. "Farmer in Inchrory. Forced out by Roderick McCulloch of Glasstulich." "Said to have come in of his own accord." *SHS.2.222, MR81.*

GARVIE, JAMES, "A common Highlander." Imprisoned 14.11.1745 Kirkliston; Edinburgh Castle, 15.1.1746 Edinburgh Tolbooth. On suspicion. Was sick with "inflammation of his utts" in April-May 1746. He was evidently deserting when caught. Released under General Pardon, 1747. *SHS.2.222.*

GILLIES or GILES, DANIEL, "Highlands", Clanranald's Regiment, imprisoned 30.12.1745 Carlisle; York Castle. Taken at capture of Carlisle, his disposal is unknown. He may have died. *SHS.2.228.*

GLASS, JOHN, aged 40, brogmakern from Milton of Red Castle, Kilernan, Ross-shire, Lord Cromarty's Regiment. Imprisoned Inverness; June 1746 prison ship *Liberty & Propety*, Medway. Transported 31.3.1747 from London to Jamaica or Barbados. Carried arms. *SHS.2.230, BMHS.30.76.*

GLASS, KENNETH, aged 45 from Cromarty, imprisoned June 1746 prison ship *Jane of Leith* Tilbury. On suspicion. His disposal is unknown. Name does not appear in transportation lists; he may have died. *SHS.2.230.*

GOLLAN, DONALD, from Avoch, Ross-shire. Transported 1747. *SHS.2.232.*

GOLLON, JOHN, from Inverness-shire, Crichton's Regiment, imprisoned Culloden; Inverness. His name only appears in the Culloden List. *SHS.2.232.*

GORDON, ALEXANDER, of Gairnside, Farquharson's Regiment, died in Inverness prison, 1746. *SHS.1.187.*

GOW, ALEXANDER, from Lochbroom, Glengarry's Regiment, imprisoned Tilbury. The minister of Lochbroom said he had been forced out. His fate is unknown. *SHS.2.244.*

GOWAN, DUNCAN (or DONALD), aged 40, farmer, parish of Aich, Ross-shire, Cromarty's Regiment, imprisoned Inverness; June 1746 prison ship *Alexander & James* Tilbury Fort, hospital ship *Liberty & Property* Medway. Transported 31.3.1747 from London to Barbados on *Frere*. *SHS.2.244, BMHS.30.77.*

GRAHAM, CHARLES, from Tain, Ross-shire, soldier in Cromerty's Regiment. Transported 31 March 1746. *SHS.2.246, BMHS.30.77.*

GRANT, ALEXANDER, of Sheuglie, aged 50, Sheuglie, Glen Urquhart, Inverness-shire. Imprisoned Inverness; June 1746 prison ship *Dolphin* Tilbury, died in prison 29.7.1746. The attitude of Sheuglie was never a clearly defined one. On his own statement he tried to prevent his men joining the Prince, and when they had gone out he claimed to have induced them to surrender after Culloden. His own chief, however, Grant of Grant, was always suspicious of him, and most treacherously had him seized and imprisoned in Inverness, as a rebel. He was sent to Tilbury, when he died of fever, 29 July 1746. *SHS.2.248.*

GRANT, ALEXANDER, aged 48, boatman from Wester Inverwick, Glenmoriston, Inverness-shire, Glengarry's Regiment. Imprisoned May 1746 Inverness; June 1746 prison ship *Dolphin* Tilbury, Tilbury Fort. Transported 29.3.1747 from London to Barbados in *Frere*. Was one of the party of 69 Grants of Glenmoriston which surrendered their arms at Inverness in May 1746 and were made prisoners. He was banished to Barbados, but managed to escape and return home about 1748. *SHS.2.248, BMHS.30.77.*

GRANT, ALEXANDER, aged 55, farmer from Wester Inverwick, Glenmoriston, Glengarry's Regiment. Imprisoned Inverness; June 1746 prison ship *Dolphin*, Aug 1746 Tilbury Fort. Transported 31.3.1747 from London to Barbados in *Frere*. "Pressed." *SHS.2.248, MR152, BMHS.30.77.*

GRANT, ALEXANDER, aged 45, farmer from Livicie, Glenmoriston, Inverness-shire, Glengarry's Regiment. Imprisoned Inverness; June 1746 prison ship *Dolphin* Tilbury, Tilbury Fort, Southwark, acquitted 16.12.1746. It is possible that this was the Alexander Grant who was brought to the Bar at St Margaret's Hill, London, on 16 December 1746. The Attorney-General pointed out that he had surrendered under the Duke's proclamation; and he was accordingly acquitted. He is described in the proceedings as "brother to Patrick Grant of Glenmoriston." *SHS.2.248.*

GRANT, ALEXANDER, aged 57, farmer from Delcaitack, Glenmoriston, Inverness-shire, Glengarry's Regiment. Imprisoned Inverness; June 1746 prison ship *Dolphin*, Tilbury Fort. Transported 20.3.1747 from London to Barbados in *Frere*. "Joined the rebel army and returned before they reached Stirling. Always bore an utter aversion to this Rebellion." *SHS.2.250, MR152.*

GRANT, ALEXANDER, aged 31, from Glen Urquhart, farmer in Glenmoriston, Inverness-shire, Glengarry's Regiment. Imprisoned Inverness; June 1746 prison ship *Dolphin* Tilbury, Tilbury Fort. Transported 31.3.1747 from London to Barbados in *Frere*. *SHS.2.250, MR152, BMHS.30.77.*

GRANT, ALEXANDER, aged 35, from Glenmoriston, Inverness-shire. Transported 31 March 1746 from London to Barbados in *Frere*. *SHS.2.250, MR152, BMHS.30.77.*

GRANT, ANGUS, aged 31, farmer in Glenmoriston, Inverness-shire, Glengarry's Regiment. Imprisoned Inverness; June 1746 prison ship *Dolphin* Tilbury Fort. Transported 30.3.1747 from London to Barbados in *Frere*. *SHS.2.250.*

GRANT, ANGUS, aged 8, from Glenmoriston, apparently the son of a man in Lochiel's Regiment, imprisoned Chester, released. *SHS.2.252.*

GRANT, ANGUS, aged 50, farmer in Glenmoriston. Transported 31 March 1746 from London to Barbados in *Frere. SHS.2.250, BMHS.30.77.*

GRANT, ARCHIBALD, aged 40, from Achtenmerak, Glen Urquhart, Inverness-shire, Glengarry's Regiment. Imprisoned Inverness; June 1746 prison ship *Dolphin* Tilbury. "Engaged willingly and went with the rebels." As his name does not appear in the transportation lists he probably died at Tilbury. *SHS.2.252, BMHS.30.77.*

GRANT, ARCHIBALD, aged 40, farmer in Glen Urquhart, Inverness-shire, Duke of Perth's Regiment. Imprisoned Inverness; Tilbury Fort. Transported 31.3.1747 from London to Barbados in *Frere. SHS.2.252, MR72.*

GRANT, DANIEL, aged 60, from Inverness, Glengarry's Regiment, imprisoned Inverness; June 1746 prison ship *Wallsgrave* Tilbury. He probably died at Tilbury. *SHS.2.252.*

GRANT, DANIEL, aged 60, from Inverness, Glengarry's Regiment, imprisoned Inverness; June 1746 prison ship *Wallsgrave* Tilbury. He probably died at Tilbury. *SHS.2.252.*

GRANT, DANIEL, aged 30, farmer in Glenmoriston, Inverness-shire, Glengarry's Regiment. Imprisoned Inverness; Tilbury Fort. No further reference to him. *SHS.2.252*

GRANT, DONALD, aged 60, from Blairy, Glenmoriston, Inverness-shire, Glengarry's Regiment. Imprisoned May 1746, Inverness; June 1746 prison ship *Wallsgrave,* Tilbury Fort. Transported 19.3.1747 to Barbados in *Frere. SHS.2.252, MR152.*

GRANT, DONALD, aged 62, farmer in Glenmoriston, Inverness-shire, Glengarry's Regiment. Imprisoned Inverness; June 1746 prison ship *Wallsgrave,* Tilbury Fort. Transported 20.3.1747. *SHS.2.252, MR152.*

GRANT, DONALD, aged 36, farmer in Balnagarn (Dalnagarn), Glenmoriston, Inverness-shire, Glengarry's Regiment. Imprisoned Inverness; June 1746 prison ship *Dolphin,* Tilbury Fort. Transported 31.3.1747 from London to Barbados. "Never in arms till pressed in March 1746 and deserted in a fortnight's time." *SHS.2.252, MR152, BMHS.30.77.*

GRANT, DONALD, aged 32, farmer from Ballintombuy, Glenmoriston, Inverness-shire, Glengarry's Regiment.

Imprisoned Inverness; June 1746 prison ship *Dolphin*, Tilbury Fort. Transported 31.3.1747 from London to Barbados in *Frere*. "Pressed twice. Upon deserting was pursued to the hills – always showed the greatest aversion to the late unnaturall rebellion." *SHS.2.254, MR152, BMHS.30.77.*

GRANT, DONALD, aged 40, farmer from Wester Dundreggan, Glenmoriston, Inverness-shire, Glengarry's Regiment. Imprisoned May 1746 Inverness; June 1746 prison ship *Dolphin*, Tilbury Fort. Transported 31.3.1747 from London to Barbados in *Frere*. A volunteer. *SHS.2.254, MR152, BMHS.30.77.*

GRANT, DONALD, aged 58, farmer in Glenmoriston, Inverness-shire, Glengarry's Regiment. Imprisoned Inverness; June 1746 prison ship *Dolphin*, Tilbury Fort. Transported from London to Barbados in *Frere*. *SHS.2.254, MR152.*

GRANT, DONALD, aged 40, farmer in Glenmoriston, Inverness-shire, Glengarry's Regiment. Imprisoned Inverness; June 1746 prison ship *Dolphin*, Tilbury Fort. Transported 31.3.1747 from Tilbury. *SHS.2.254, BMHS.30.77.*

GRANT, DUGAL, aged 11 from Glenmoriston, Inverness-shire. Imprisoned Carlisle and Chester, released. *SHS.2.254.*

GRANT, DUGAL, aged 50, farmer in Glenmoriston, Inverness-shire, Glengarry's Regiment. Imprisoned May 1746 Inverness; ilbury Fort. Transported 31.3.1747 from London to Barbados in *Frere*. *SHS.2.254, MR154, BMHS.30.77.*

GRANT, DUNCAN, aged 45, farmer in Wester Dundreggan, Glenmoriston, Inverness-shire, Glengarry's Regiment. Imprisoned May 1746 Inverness; June 1746 prison ship *Dolphin* Tilbury Fort. Transported 20.3.1747 from Tilbury. *SHS.2.254, MR152.*

GRANT, DUNCAN, aged 34 from Livicie, Glenmoriston, Inverness-shire, Glengarry's Regiment. Imprisoned Inverness; June 1746 prison ship *Dolphin* Tilbury Fort, discharged. Servant to Patrick Grant. *SHS.2.254.*

GRANT, FARQUHAR, aged 43, farmer in Glenmoriston, Inverness-shire, Glengarry's Regiment. Imprisoned Inverness; June 1746 prison ship *Wallsgrave*, Tilbury. Transported 20.3.1747. *SHS.2.254, MR152.*

GRANT, FARQUHAR, Glengarry's Regiment, imprisoned Inverness; Tilbury. Transported 31.3.1747. *SHS.2.254.*

GRANT, GEORGE, aged 40, farmer in Glenmoriston, Inverness-shire, Glengarry's Regiment. Imprisoned Inverness; June

1746 prison ship *Dolphin*, Aug 1746 Tilbury Fort. Transported 31.3.1747 from London to Barbados in *Frere*. *SHS.2.256, MR152, BMHS.30.77.*

GRANT, HUGH, aged 50, farmer in Glenmoriston, Inverness-shire, Glengarry's Regiment. Imprisoned Inverness; June 1746 prison ship *Dolphin*, Aug 1746 Tilbury Fort. Transported 31.3.1747 from London to Barbados in *Frere*. *SHS.2.256, BMHS.30.77.*

GRANT, HUGH, aged 35, husbandman from Glenmoriston, Gengarry's Regiment. Imprisoned Inverness; June 1746 prison ship *Dolphin*, Tilbury Fort. His disposal is unknown. *SHS.2.256.*

GRANT, JAMES, of Sheuglie, younger. Of Sheuglie, Urquhart, Inverness-shire. Imprisoned Inverness; London. Discharged on bail Sept 1746; again discharged Edinburgh 4.12.1746. Son of Alexander Grant of Sheuglie. Shared with his father the suspicion of his chief, Grant of Grant, and was made prisoner by Grant's orders, and lodged in Inverness. He was sent to London, where he was examined. He insisted that he and his father had tried to help the Government, and had suffered in his property at the hands of his own men. On the recommendation of the Attorney-General and Solicitor-General he was discharged on bail, to stand his trial in Edinburgh in December 1746, when witnesses on both sides would be available. When this trial came on he and the Rev John Grant were again admitted to bail. *SHS.2.256.*

GRANT, JAMES, Revd, aged 40, a priest. Imprisoned Barra; Inverness, June 1746 prison ship *Jane of Alloway*, released July 1747. *SHS.2.256.*

GRANT, JAMES, of Locheleter, aged 61, farmer in Wester Inverwick, Glenmoriston, Glengarry's Regiment. Imprisoned Inverness; June 1746 prison ship *Dolphin*, Aug 1746 Tilbury Fort. Transported 1747 from Tilbury. "Resisted all sollicitations till forced to the North in March, but soon returned." *SHS.2.258.*

GRANT, JAMES, aged 50 (45), farmer in Blairy, Glenmoriston, Inverness-shire, Glengarry's Regiment. Imprisoned May 1746 Inverness; June 1746 prison ship *Wallsgrave* Tilbury, Tilbury Fort. Transported 31.3.1747 from London to Barbados in *Frere*. "Forced in March last but soon deserted." *SHS.2.258, MR153, BMHS.30.77.*

GRANT, JOHN, Revd, aged 34, from Glen Urquhart, Inverness-shire. Imprisoned 9.5.1746 Inverness; June 1746 prison ship *Dolphin* Tilbury, London (Tilbury), discharged on bail Spet 1746, again discharged Edinburgh 4.12.1746. He was "Minister of the Gospel in Urquhart." He was accused of "explaining the Pretender's Manifesto from the Pulpit." This he denied, and claimed to have acted on the side of the Government throughout, and to have suffered grievously at the hands of the McDonalds in consequence. His own chief, Ludovic Grant, suspected him and had him taken prisoner, and in due course he was sent to London with the Grants of Sheuglie. He gave evidence in his own favour in London in august 1746 and was discharged on bail, to stand trial in Edinburgh in the following December; there he was again discharged. *SHS.1.223, SHS.2.258.*

GRANT, JOHN, aged 40, farmer from Craskie, Glenmoriston, Inverness-shire, Glengarry's Regiment. Imprisoned Inverness; June 1746 prison ship *Wallsgrave* Tilbury, Tilbury Fort. Transported 31.3.1747 from London to Barbados in *Frere*. Deserted from the Prince's army before prestonpans. Again forced in November 1745 but deserted from Perth. Surrendered 5 May 1746. *SHS.2.258, MR153, BMHS.30.77.*

GRANT, JOHN, aged 45, farmer in Belnagarn, Glenmoriston, Inverness-shire, Glengarry's Regiment. He twice deserted. Imprisoned Inverness; June 1746 prison ship *Wallsgrave* Tilbury, Tilbury Fort. Transported 31.3.1747 from London to Barbados in *Frere*. *SHS.2.260, MR153, BMHS.30.77.*

GRANT, JOHN, aged 38, farmer in Inverwick, Glenmoriston, Inverness-shire, Glengarry's Regiment. "Of a valueable character and always showed a marked aversion to rebellion tho obliged to be in arms." Imprisoned Inverness; June 1746 prison ship *Dolphin*, Tilbury Fort. Transported 20.3.1747 (31.3.1747?) from London to Barbados in *Frere*. *SHS.2.260, MR153.*

GRANT, JOHN, aged 41, farmer in Easter Achlein, Glenmoriston, Inverness-shire, Glengarry's Regiment. "Pressed, and still deserted." Imprisoned Inverness; June 1746 prison ship *Dolphin*, Tilbury Fort. Transported 31.3.1747 from London to Barbados in *Frere*. *SHS.2.260, MR153, BMHS.30.78.*

GRANT, JOHN, aged 50, farmer in Glenmoriston, Inverness-shire, Glengarry's Regiment. Imprisoned Inverness; June 1746 prison ship *Wallsgrave* Tilbury, Tilbury Fort. Transported

31.3.1747 from London to Barbados in *Frere. SHS.2.260, MR153, BMHS.30.78.*
GRANT, JOHN, aged 30, farmer in Glenmoriston, Inverness-shire, Glengarry's Regiment. Imprisoned Inverness; June 1746 prison ship *Dolphin,* Tilbury Fort. Transported 31.3.1747 from London to Barbados in *Frere. SHS.2.260, MR153, BMHS.30.78.*
GRANT, JOHN, aged 40, farmer in Glenmoriston, Inverness-shire, Glengarry's Regiment. Imprisoned Inverness; June 1746 prison ship *Dolphin,* Tilbury Fort. Transported 31.3.1747 from London to Barbados in *Frere. SHS.2.260, MR153, BMHS.30.78.*
GRANT, JOHN, aged 25,farmer in Glenmoriston, Inverness-shire,Glengarry's Regiment. Imprisoned Inverness; June 1746 prison ship *Dolphin,* Tilbury Fort. Transported 31.3.1747 from London to Barbados in *Frere. SHS.2.260, MR153, BMHS.30.78.*
GRANT, JOHN, aged 40, farmer in Glenmoriston, Inverness-shire,Glengarry's Regiment. Imprisoned Inverness; June 1746 prison ship *Dolphin,* Tilbury Fort. Transported 31.3.1747 from London to Barbados in *Frere. SHS.2.260, MR153, BMHS.30.78.*
GRANT, JOHN, aged 55,farmer in Glen Urquhart, Inverness-shire,Glengarry's Regiment. Imprisoned Inverness; June 1746 prison ship *Dolphin,* Tilbury Fort. Transported 31.3.1747 from London to Barbados in *Frere. SHS.2.260, MR153.*
GRANT, JOHN, aged 45,farmer in Glenmoriston, Inverness-shire,Glengarry's Regiment. Imprisoned Inverness; June 1746 prison ship *Dolphin,* Tilbury Fort. Transported 31.3.1747 from London to Barbados in *Frere. SHS.2.260, MR153, BMHS.30.78.*
GRANT, JOHN, aged 22, from Glenmoriston, Inverness-shire,Glengarry's Regiment. Imprisoned Inverness; June 1746 prison ship *Dolphin,* Tilbury Fort. Transported 31.3.1747 from London to Barbados in *Frere. SHS.2.260, MR153, BMHS.30.78.*
GRANT, JOHN, aged 26,farmer in Glenmoriston, Inverness-shire, Glengarry's Regiment. Imprisoned Inverness; June 1746 prison ship *Wallsgrave,* Tilbury Fort. Transported 31.3.1747 from London to Barbados in *Frere. SHS.2.260, MR153, BMHS.30.78.*

GRANT, JOHN, aged 23, from Glenmoriston, Inverness-shire, Glengarry's Regiment. Imprisoned Inverness; June 1746 prison ship *Wallsgrave*, Tilbury Fort. Transported 31.3.1747 from Tilbury. *SHS.2.260.*

GRANT, JOHN, "Common Highlander, a boy, attending the rebels." From Glenmoriston, Inverness-shire, Glengarry's Regiment. Imprisoned 4.11.1745 Duddingston; Edinburgh Castle, 15.1.1746 Edinburgh, 8.8.1746 Carlisle, York Castle. Transported 1747. *SHS.2.262, MR153.*

GRANT, JOHN, aged 40, labourer from Badenoch or Lochaber, Invernessshire, taken at capture of Carlisle, Lochiel's Regiment. Imprisoned 30.12.1745 Carlisle; York Castle. Transported 8.5.1747 from Liverpool to Leeward Islands, in *Veteran*, arriving Martiniquew June 1747. *SHS.2.262, MR35, PRO.SP36.102.*

GRANT, PATRICK, aged 47, farmer in Glenmoriston, Inverness-shire, Glengarry's Regiment. Imprisoned Inverness; Tilbury Fort. No further reference to him. He probably died. *SHS.2.262.*

GRANT, PATRICK, aged 30, farmer in Glenmoriston, Inverness-shire, Glengarry's Regiment. Imprisoned Inverness; Tilbury Fort. Transported 1747 from Tilbury. *SHS.2.262, MR153.*

GRANT, PATRICK, aged 45, farmer in Glenmoriston, Inverness-shire, Glengarry's Regiment. Imprisoned Inverness; Tilbury Fort. No further reference to him. He probably died. *SHS.2.262.*

GRANT, PETER, aged 50, farmer from Tullocherchait Mor, Glenmoriston, Inverness-shire,Glengarry's Regiment. Imprisoned Inverness; prison ship *Wallsgrave* Tilbury, Tilbury Fort. Transported 31.3.1747 from London to Barbados in *Frere*. *SHS.2.262, MR153, BMHS.30.78.*

GRANT, PETER, aged 46, from Easter Achlein, Glenmoriston, Inverness-shire. "Pressed." Glengarry's Regiment, Imprisoned Inverness; June 1746 prison ship *Dolphin*, Tilbury Fort. Transported 20.3.1747 from Tilbury. *SHS.2.264, MR153.*

GRANT, PETER, aged 24, fiddler in Glen Urquhart, Inverness-shire, Glengarry's Regiment. Imprisoned Inverness; June 1746 prison ship *Dolphin*, hospital ship *Liberty & Property*, Medway. Transported 31.3.1747 from London to Jamaica in *St George or Carteret*, arriving Jamaica 1747. *SHS.2.264, PRO.CO137.58, BMHS.30.78.*

GRANT, WILLIAM, aged 45, from Inverness, Roy Stuart's Regiment. Imprisoned Inverness; June 1746 prison ship *Margaret & Mary*, Tilbury. Transported 1747. *SHS.2.264, MR206.*

GRANT, WILLIAM, from Carnach, Glen Urquhart, Inverness-shire. "Forced. An honest man." Glengarry's Regiment. Imprisoned 6.5.1746 Inverness, Tilbury. Transported 1747. He was one of the very few who managed to return to Scotland. He became tenant of Breakry-riach. *SHS.2.264, MR153.*

GRASSICK, JOHN, from Inverness-shire, Lord Lovat's Regiment. Imprisoned Culloden; Inverness. Name in Culloden List. No further reference to him. He probably died. *SHS.2.264.*

GRAY, JOHN, aged 40, from Sutherland, Captain, Lord John Drummond's French Service. Imprisoned Culloden; Inverness, June 1746 *Jane of Leith*, London (Southwark), pardoned on condition of permanent banishment 2.7.1747. Mrs Leith, in Inverness, describes him as "a gentleman of a small estate in Sutherland who had been a few years only serving in France." He was regarded as a French prisoner of war. In a letter to Mrs Leith, dated 28 June 1746, he complained of being confined in fetters weighing 40 lbs. *SHS.2.266.*

GUN, ANGUS, aged 20, husbandman in Lairn in Caithness, Cromary's Regiment. Imprisoned Inverness; June 1746 prison ship *Thane of Fife,* and *James & Mary* Tilbury. Transported 20.3.1747 from London to Jamaica or Barbados, arriving Jamaica 1747. *SHS.2.270, MR82, PRO.CO137.28, BMHS.30.78.*

GUN, DANIEL, aged 30, from Caithness, imprisoned "on suspicion" Inverness; prison ship *Margaret & Mary.* Transported 31.3.1747. *SHS.2.270.*

GUN, DONALD, aged 30, from Caithness, Cromarty's Regiment. Imprisoned Inverness; prison ship *James & Mary* Medway. Transported 31.3.1747 from London to Jamaica or Barbados. *SHS.2.270.*

GUN, DONALD, aged 40, husbandman from Dunbeath Caithness, Cromarty's Regiment. Imprisoned Inverness; June 1746 hospital ship *Liberty & Property* Medway. Transported 31.3.1747. *SHS.2.272, MR82, PRO.CO137.58, BMHS.30.78.*

HARPER, JOHN (or JAMES), staymaker and tailor from Inverness. Imprisoned on suspicion Inverness; June 1746 prison ship

Margaret & Mary, hospital ship Liberty & Property. He probably died at Tilbury. SHS.2.276.

HAY, JOHN, from Inverness. Imprisoned Inverness; London (Southwark), discharged. This was probably the man who gave evidence against Lord Macleod and others. SHS.2.280

HENDERSON, JOHN, of Castlemains, Lochmaben, Writer. Imprisoned Carlisle Castle, executed at Carlisle 21.10.1746. "Was committed at Carlisle for drinking treasonable healths; set at liberty and made Jail Keeper by the Rebels on their getting possession of that place; made his escape when HRH the Duke of Cumberland retook that city, and now since Culloden has been apprehended and is prisoner in Carlisle." He was subsequently tried and sentenced to death, and executed. SHS.2.284.

HOOD, ANDREW, aged 20, apprentice from Tain, Ross-shire, Cromarty's Regiment. Imprisoned Inverness; Tilbury Fort. Transported 19.3.1747. SHS.2.290, MR82.

JACK, ANDREW, aged 30, from Caithness, Cromarty's Regiment. Imprisoned Inverness; June 1746 prison ship Thane of Fife Tilbury. Transported 20.3.1747 from London to Jamaica or Barbados in St George or Carteret, arriving Jamaica 1747. SHS.2.298, MR82, PRO.CO137.58, BMHS.30.78.

JACK or JACKES, DUNCAN (or DONALD), aged 58, beggar from Ross. "On suspicion." Imprisoned Inverness; June 1746 prison ship Jane of Leith Tilbury. Transported 20.3.1747 from London to Jamaica or Barbados. SHS.2.300.

JACQUE, ANDREW, aged 30, husbandman from Ross or Elgin, Cromarty's Regiment. Imprisoned Inverness; prison ship James & Mary Tilbury. Transported 1747 from Tilbury. SHS.2.300.

JACQUE, DONALD, aged 58, a beggar, on suspicion, formerly an ale seller in Avoch" from Ross-shire. Imprisoned Inverness; Tilbury Fort. Transported 20.3.1747 from London to Jamaica or Barbados. SHS.2.300 (see JACK).

JOHNSTON, or JOHNSON, JOHN, aged 13, from Argyllshire. Imprisoned Inverness; June 1746 prison ship Margaret & Mary Tilbury. Servant to a French officer. No further reference to him, he may have died. SHS.2.304.

KENNEDY, ALEXANDER, from Glenkine, Glengarry, Inverness-shire, Glengarry's Regiment. Imprisoned 4.11.1745 Duddingston; 15.1.1746 Edinburgh Jail, released under General Pardon, 1747. SHS.2.312.

KENNEDY, ANGUS ROY, from Mull. Imprisoned "County of Argyll" on suspicion. Denies he was in the rebellion. Can given no distinct account of himself. Is guilty of habitual stealing. *SHS.2.312.*

KENNEDY, or KENADY, ANGUS, aged 13, Shean, Inverness-shire. Imprisoned Carlisle; Chester Castle. This boy, and the next, were perhaps the sons of the Mary Kennedy who was taken at Carlisle and transported. Their fate is not known, but they probably went with her. *SHS.2.312.*

KENNEDY, or KENADY, ANGUS, aged 10, Shean, Inverness-shire. Imprisoned Carlisle; Chester Castle. See above. *SHS.2.312.*

KENNEDY, DONALD, from Rannoch, Glengarry's Regiment. Imprisoned 1.2.1746 Stirling; 13.2.1746 Canongate; 8.8.1746 Carlisle. With "baggage horse." Does not appear to have been transported. Disposal unknown. *SHS.2.314.*

KENNEDY, DOUGAL, from Herdboy from Rannoch. Imprisoned 1.2.1746 Stirling; 7.2.1746 Stirling Castle, 13.2.1746 Leith, discharged. "With baggage horse." *SHS.2.314.*

KENNEDY, DUNCAN, from Rannoch, Glengarry's Regiment. Imprisoned Stirling; 7.2.1746 Stirling Castle, discharged. Attended to baggage. Probably this and the above two were related. *SHS.2.314.*

KENNEDY, ENIS, from the "Highlands", McPherson's Regiment. Imprisoned 30.12.1745 Carlisle. Taken at capture of Carlisle. No further reference to him. He may have died in prison. *SHS.2.314.*

KENNEDY, JOHN, aged 20, cowherd at Dougin, Inverness-shire, Glengarry's Regiment. Imprisoned Inverness; Sept 1746 *Pamela* Tilbury, transported 31.3.1747 from London to Barbados in *Frere. SHS.2.314, MR154, BMHS.30.78.*

KENNEDY, JOHN, labourer from Kilenan, Glengarry, Inverness-shire, Shian McDonal's (Glengarry's) Regiment. Imprisoned 4.11.1745 Duddingston; 25.1.1746 Edinburgh Jail, discharged. In hospital with pain in ears. "Says he was forced to serve Shian McDonald in the rebel army as a baggage man and deserted at Dalkeith." *SHS.2.316.*

KENNEDY, MARY, and child, aged 20, from Glengarry, Inverness-shire, Glengarry's Regiment, sews "sews and washes." Imprisoned Carlisle; York Castle, Chester. Transported 5 May 1747 from Liverpool to Leeward Islands in Veteran, arrived Martinique June 1747. *SHS.2.316, PRO.SP36.102.*

KERR or KER, AENEAS, aged 40, from Ross-shire, Cromarty's Regiment. Imprisoned Inverness; June 1746 prison ship *Wallsgrave* Tilbury. He was not transported, so he probably died. *SHS.2.316.*

KERR, DONALD, aged 35, farmer from Aghnagaird, Ross-shire, Cromarty's Regiment. Imprisoned Inverness; Tilbury Fort, transported 20.3.1747 from Tilbury. *SHS.2.318, MR82.*

KINASTON, JOHN, from Lochaber, Inverness-shire, Kilmarnocks' Regiment. Imprisoned Inverness. "John Gilmour say he was billeted on him, while the rebels were at his house, and that he told him he belonged to Kilmarnock's regiment." There is no further reference to him. He may have died in one of the transports. *SHS.2.320.*

LINEN, JOHN, from Skye. Imprisoned Dumbarton Castle, released under General Pardon, 1747. *SHS.2.344.*

LIVINGSTON, JOHN, Founder, from Ardnamurchan, Argyllshire, McGregor's, Glengyle's Regiment. Imprisoned 15.11.1745 Ardno; 17.12.1745 Dumbarton, liberated 21.8.1747. *SHS.2.346.*

LOVAT, Lord SIMON FRASER, aged 79, from Inverness-shire. Imprisoned 11.12.1745 Castle Downie; 1746 Loch Morar Inverness, Fort William, Tower of London, beheaded Tower Hill 9.4.1747. Born about 1667, Simon Fraser, 11th Lord Fraser of Lovat, one of the most remarkable men of his day. At the outbreak of the Rising he offered his services to the Prince and sent his son to join him, while he himself remained at home. After Prestonpans he raised his clan, but on 11 December was taken by Lord Loudoun and held as hostage for their fidelity. From this captivity he escaped with the help of Mrs Leith. After Culloden he met the Prince at Gortuleg and tried to induce him to make another stand, and on his refusal retired to a hiding-place. He was hunted about and ultimately captured at Loch Morar. He was carried in a litter to Fort William and thence sent to London, to the Tower. He was tried before the House of Lords for high treason and condemned to death on 18 March 1747. He appealed for mercy, but the appeal was refused. The sentence of beheading was carried out on 9 April 1747. He was then 80 years of age. *SHS.2.348.*

LOVAT, Master of, SIMON FRASER, aged 20, Castle Downy, Kiltarlity, Inverness-shire, "One of the chief commanders of the Frasers." Imprisoned 10.8.1746 Fort Augustus, surrendered to Lord Loudoun; 10.8.1746 Inverness, Nov

1746 Edinburgh Castle, 7.8.1747 Glasgow, attainted July 1746, pardoned 1750. Born 19 Oct 1726, he was the eldest son of Simon Fraser, 11th Lord Lovat. He raised and led the Clan Fraser and was present at Falkirk and Culloden. His corps numbered about 300 men. After Culloden he surrendered to Loudoun on 10 August. On his father's execution on 9 April 1747 he became *de jure* 12th Lord Fraser of Lovat, but, owing to the attainder of 1746, did not succeed to the honours or estate. On 15.8.1747 he was ordered to go to Glasgow and to stay there until the King's pleasure regarding him was signified to him. He was pardoned in 1750 and became an Advocate. In 1757 he raised and became Colonel of the Fraser Highlanders, and served with it in America under Wolfe, and was twice wounded. In 1762 he was sent as Brigadier-General to Portugal. In 1774 his forfeited estates were returned to him on payment of £21,000. In 1776 he raised two more Highland battalions. He died 8 Feb 1782. *SHS.2.350.*

LOW, ROGER or RODERICK, from Ross-shire, Duke of Perth's Regiment. Imprisoned Inverness; Sept 1746 prison ship *Pamela* Tilbury. Transported 30.3.1747 from London to Jamaica in *St George or Carteret*, arriving Jamaica 1747. "Servant to Lord Cromartie at Tarbat House. *SHS.2.352, BMHS.30.79.*

MARCHAND, JOHN, aged 24 from Inverness, Lochiel's Regiment. Imprisoned Inverness; June 1746 prison ship *Alexander & James*. Not shown in transportation lists; possibly died. *SHS.3.8.*

MASTERTON, MALCOLM, from Inverness, McIntosh's Regiment. Imprisoned Culloden, Inverness. See Culloden List. No further reference to him in London or elsewhere. He probably died. *SHS.3.10.*

MATHIESON or MATHEWSON, KENNETH, aged 26 from Ross, Cromarty's Regiment. Imprisoned Inverness; Tilbury Fort. Transported 31.3.1747 from London to Barbados in *Frere*. Servant to his brother Finlay in Strathpeffer. *SHS.3.12, MR82, BMHS.30.79.*

MONROE, ALAN, aged 28, farmer in Glenmoriston, Inverness-shire, Glengarry's Regiment. Imprisoned Inverness, June 1746 prison ship *Dolphin*, Tilbury Fort. Transported 31.3.1747 from London to Barbados in *Frere*. *SHS.3.204, MR159, BHMS.84.*

MONRO, DONALD, from Dunrobin, Cromarty's Regiment. Imprisoned Dunrobin, Inverness, Tilbury. Discharged. He gave evidence against his commanding officer, Lord MacLeod. *SHS.3.204.*

MONRO, HECTOR, aged 31, drummer from Ross-shire, deserted from Loudoun's Regiment. Imprisoned Inverness, June 1746 prison ship *Alexander & James,* hospital ship *Liberty & Property.* Transported 31.3.1747 from London to Jamaica in *St George or Carteret,* arriving Jamaica 1747. *SHS.3.206, PRO.CO137.58, BHMS.84.*

MONRO, WILLIAM, aged 70, from Inverness-shire, Clanranald's Regiment. Imprisoned Culloden, Inverness, June 1746 prison ship *Wallsgrave.* Died. See Culloden List. *SHS.3.206.*

MORRISON, ALEXANDER, aged 50, from distiller from Isle of Lewis, resident in Mull, Argyll, McLachlan's Regiment. Imprisoned Inverness, June 1746 prison ship *Alexander & James,* hospital ship *Liberty,* Medway. Transported 31.3.1747 from London to Barbados in *Frere. SHS.3.210, MR181, BHMS.84.*

MOUCHALL, ANDREW, from Inverness-shire, Lovat's Regiment. Imprisoned Culloden, Inverness. Died. *SHS.3.214.*

MURRAY, GEORGE, Kilmarnock's Horse, died at sea on prison ship *Jane of Leith,* 20 May 1746. *SHS.1.188.*

MACALISTER, ARCHIBALD, from Glengarry, Inverness-shire. Imprisoned "on suspicion" Glengowlandy, Apnadull, Perth, discharged on bail 31.7.1746. *SHS.3.18.*

McARTHUR or McCARTER, JOHN, Brewer from Inverness, Roy Stuart's Regiment. Imprisoned 30.12.1745 Carlisle, York Castle. "Carried arms and went to England." His fate is not known. *SHS.3.18.*

MACAULAY, ANGUS, aged 22 from Benbecula. Imprisoned HMS *Furnace*; London. Released 11.6.1747. Servant to Benbecula. Turned King's Evidence. He was in the house of Dick the messenger for a year, and was never brought to trial. On 11 June 1747 he was released. *SHS.3.18.*

McAULAY, NEIL, itinerant tailor from North Uist, Lovat's Regiment. Imprisoned HMS *Furnace*; Sept 1746 prison ship *Pamela,* Oct 1746 Tilbury, released 25.5.1747. "Capt Ferguson reports he was guilty of many acts of barbarity and was to be employed by Barrisdale to undertake the murder of him." Against his name is stated: "Evidence against Lord Lovat."

He was still in Tilbury Fort in April 1747. He was released after Lovat's execution. *SHS.3.19.*

McBANE, DONALD, aged 28 from Inverness, McIntosh's Regiment. Imprisoned Inverness; June 1746 prison ship *Alexander & James.* There is no further refeence to him. He may have died. *SHS.3.20.*

McBAIN, DUNCAN or DONALD, aged 30, husbandman by the reiver Nairn, Inverness-shire, Cromarty's (McIntosh's?) Regiment. Imprisoned Inverness; HMS *Liberty,* Medway. Transported 1747. *SHS.3.20, MR174.*

McBAIN, JAMES, aged 49 from Petty, Inverness. Imprisoned Inverness; June 1746 prison ship *Jane of Leith,* Tilbury Fort, transported 20.3.1747 from Tilbury. "Apprehended on suspicion. Parochial catechist, Parish of Petty." *SHS.3.20.*

McBAIN, JOHN, aged 44 from Inverness-shire, McIntosh's Regiment. Imprisoned Inverness; June 1746 prison ship *Jane of Leith.* No further reference to him. May have died. *SHS.3.20.*

McBAIN, WILLIAM, from Inverness, McIntosh's Regiment. Imprisoned Inverness; June 1746 prison ship *Jane of Leith,* died sea on *Jane of Leith,* 28 May 1746. *SHS.187, SHS.3.20.*

McCALLUM, JOHN, from Inverness-shire, Glengyle's Regiment. Imprisoned 15.11.1745 Ardon; 17.12.1747 Dumbarton, discharged. "Tenant to McKinnan." *SHS.3.22.*

McCALLUM, RODERICK, from Lochbroom. Imprisoned Tilbury. The minister of Lochbroom petitioned for him that he had been forced out. His fate is unknown. *SHS.3.22.*

McCAMEL, JOHN, from Argyll, McDonald's Regiment. Imprisoned 30.12.1745 Carlisle. Taken at capture of Carlisle. There is no further reference to him. *SHS.3.22.*

McCAY, or MACKVEE *alias* **CAMERON, EWEN,** from Lochiel. Imprisoned Oct 1746 Inverness, died Nov 1746. "One of the McCays of Ha, an old tribe of McIntoshes." Was taken in Lord Seaforth's country carrying documents written in French. He was sent to Inverness, and received 500 lashes, which was repeated some days later. He refused to give any information. He died in prison." *SHS.3.24.*

McCAY, WILLIAM, aged 20, from Caithness, Cromarty's Regiment. Imprisoned Inverness; June 1746 prison ship *Thane of Fife.* No further reference to him. He may have died. *SHS.3.24.*

McCLELOR, ALEXANDER, aged 28, from Ross-shire, Cromarty's Regiment. Imprisoned Inverness; June 1746 prison ship *Wallsgrave*. No fruther reference to him; he may have died. *SHS.3.24.*

McCLUNALD, JOHN, aged 30, from Inverness-shire, Glengarry's Regiment. Imprisoned Inverness; June 1746 prison ship *Thane of Fife*. No further reference to him. *SHS.3.24.*

McCLURY, JOHN, aged 60, from Argyllshire, McLachlan's Regiment. Imprisoned Inverness; June 1746 prison ship *Alexander & James*. No further reference to him, probably died. *SHS.3.24.*

McCOIG *alias* McLACHLAN, PATRICK, from Ballimore, Lorn, Argyllshire, McLachlan's Regiment. Surrendered June 1746 Inveraray; imprisoned Dumbarton Castle, 4.2.1747 Glasgow, discharged 15.7.1747. Servant with John McLachlan. "Served under McLachlan of that ilk after the battle of Culloden and was apprehended at Lochowside." *SHS.3.26.*

McCOLL, HUGH, from Aros, Mull. Imprisoned Canongate; 8.8.1746 Carlisle. No further trace of him. *SHS.3.26.*

McCOLL, JOHN, sen, from Appin, Ardshiel's Regiment. Imprisoned May 1746 Appin; May 1746 Dumbarton Castle, 4.2.1747 Glasgow, discharged 15.7.1747. "Joined the rebels after the battle of Falkirk. Apprehended in Appin after Culloden by the Argyllshire levies." *SHS.3.26.*

McCOLL, JOHN, jun, from Appin, Ardshiel's Regiment. Imprisoned May 1746 Appin; May 1746 Dumbarton Castle, 4.2.1747 Glasgow, discharged 15.7.1747. Servant to Mrs Steuart of Fasnacloich. "Joined the rebels after the battle of Falkirk. Apprehended in Appin after Culloden by the Argyllshire levies." *SHS.3.26.*

McCOLL, JOHN, from Portnacrosh (Port-na-Croish), Appin, "an officer in the rebel army." Imprisoned Canongate; 8.8.1746 Carlisle. Son of a brewer. No further reference to him. *SHS.3.26.*

McCOLL, SAMUEL, sen, from Appin. Imprisoned May 1746 Appin; Dumbarton Castle, discharged. "Was found stealing in General Campbell's camp in Appin in the night time and was apprehended as a spy. Denies he was in the rebellion." *SHS.3.26.*

McCOLL, SAMUEL, from Appin, Ardshiel's Regiment. Imprisoned May 1746 Appin; Dumbarton Castle, discharged. "Was apprehended along with the other Samuel McDoll. Was in the rebellion and delivered up his arms and surrendered some few days before he attempted to get into the camp." *SHS.3.26.*

McCOLL, SAMUEL, from Appin, Ardshiel's Regiment. Imprisoned May 1746 Appin; May 1746 Dumbarton Castle, 4.2.1747 Glasgow. Discharged 15.4.1747. "Joined the rebels on their return from England, as at the battles of Falkirk and Culloden." *SHS.3.26.*

McCORMACK, ANGUS, Clanranald's Regiment, imprisoned 30.12.1746 Carlisle. Taken at capture of Carlisle. No further reference to him. *SHS.3.28.*

McCORMICK, DONALD, from Appin. Imprisoned Canongate; 8.8.1746 Carlisle, acquitted 19.9.1746. Was tried at Carlisle 19/26 Sept 1746, and acquitted. *SHS.3.28.*

McCORMICK, JOHN, from Appin. Imprisoned July 1746 Royal Infirmary; Canongate, discharged. Tailor in Appin. "Declares that he never carried arms of joined the rebels but came to Edinburgh to see his brother who was wounded at Preston and there made prisoner." *SHS.3.28.*

McCORMICK, MARK, aged 16, labourer from Moidart. Imprisoned Carlisle; York Castle. Transported from Liverpool to Antigua 8.5.1747 in *Veteran*, arriving Martinique June 1747. *SHS.3.28, PRO.SP36.120.*

McCORMACK, ROBERT, aged 40, farmer, Clatill, Eigg, Inverness-shire, Clanranald's Regiment. Imprisoned Inverness; Sept 1746 prison ship *Pamela*, Tilbury. Transported 31.3.1747 from London to Jamaica in *St George or Carteret*, arriving Jamaica 1747. *SHS.3.28, PRO.CO137.58, MR141, BMHS.30.79.*

McCULLEN (McCallum), JAMES, from Grantly, Roy Stuart's Regiment. Taken at capture of Carlisle, imprisoned 30.12.1745 Carlisle. No further reference to him. *SHS.3.30.*

McCULLOCH, RODERICK, of Glastullich, Easter Ross, Captain, Cromarty's Regiment. Imprisoned 15.4.1746 Dunrobin; HMS *Hound*, London (Southwark), pardoned 10.5.1748. A vassel of the Earl of Cromarty. He was taken to London, pleaded guilty when tried, but was not sentenced. At his trial evidence was produced by English officers of his humanity while they were prisoners at Perth, and he was said to have helped a surgeon's mate to escape after the battle of Falkirk. In May 1748 he received a free pardon. *Scots Mag April 1746, 190; SHS.3.32.*

McCULLOCH, SAMUEL, from Appin, Argyllshire. Baggage carrier to Stewart of Invernahyle. Imprisoned 2.2.1746 Doune; 7.2.1746 Stirling Castle, 13.2.1746 Leith, Canongate, 8.8.1746 Carlisle. In hospital with scurvy. No further reference to him. He probably died. *SHS.3.32.*

McDANIEL, PETER, from Inverness, Glenbucket's Regiment. Imprisoned 30.12.1745 Carlisle. Taken at capture of Carlisle. No further reference to him. *SHS.3.32.*

McDONALD, AENEAS, sen, from Moidart, Clanranald's Regiment. Imprisoned Edinburgh Castle; 15.1.1746 Edinburgh Jail, discharged. "Common highlander." On suspicion. *SHS.3.34.*

McDONALD, AENEAS, jun, from Moidart, Clanranald's Regiment. Imprisoned Edinburgh Castle; 15.1.1746 Edinburgh, dischrged. "Common highlander." On suspicion. *SHS.3.36.*

McDONALD of Boisdale, ALEXANDER. Imprisoned June 1746 Boisdale; London (Tilbury), London (in a Messenger's House), released 4.7.1747. Half brother to Ranald Macdonald of Clanranald. When the Prince landed in Eriska on 23 July 1745 Boisdale refused to assist him, implored the Prince to go back, and prevented Clanranald's islesmen from joining him. For this he was thanked for the services he had rendered to the Government. He visited the Prince when he was hiding in Coradale. He was taken prisoner in June 1746 and taken to London, and was only released a year later. The Privy Council directed that he be tried in Scotland, but the Indemnity saved him. *SHS.3.36.*

McDONALD, ALEXANDER of "Garigole" (Geridhoil), South Uist imprisoned London Tilbury, released April 1747. Tacksman of the McDonald's of Morar. "Was implicated in the Prince's escape, taken prisoner and taken to London as evidence against old lady Clanranald." This may be the man of whom it was stated that "by mistake he was apprehended for the servant of the Bailie." There is no doubt he turned King's Evidence. *SHS.3.36.*

McDONALD, ALEXANDER, of Glencoe, Captain (?Lieutenant Colonel), Keppoch's Regiment. Imprisoned 12.5.1746 Glencoe, surrendered to General Campbell, and was sent to Inveraray on parole; 6.3.1747 Edinburgh Castle, June 1749 Edinburgh Tolbooth. Released 11.10.1749. Chief of the McDonalds of Glencoe. McDonald of Glencoe was one of the first to visit the Prince when he landed in Scotland. He raised 120 men and joined him on 27 August. He served on the Prince's Council during the operations. After Culloden he and his men on 12 May 1746 surrendered to General Campbell and gave up their arms. In the report on this General Campbell says Glencoe said they had 52 killed and 36 wounded. On 15 May he appealed to have an interview with Cumberland as soon as he was fit to travel. He was sent on parole to Inveraray until 6 March 1747, when he went to Edinburgh; he was then taken to Edinburgh Castle and subsequently to Edinburgh Tolbooth. He was excepted from the Act of Pardon of June 1747, and remained in prison until 11 Oct 1749, when he was released by a Judge of the Court of Justiciary, in ursuance of his application "made .... In terms of our Habeas Corpus Act of 1701." His later history has not been traced. *SHS.3.38.*

McDONALD or MacDONELL of Glengarry, ALEXANDER. Imprisoned at sea December 1745; Tower of London. Rleased and exiled, 1747. "Alastair ruadh." "Young Glengarry." Eldest son of John McDonell of Glengarry, and presumably "Pickle the Spy." He had been sent by certain chiefs to France in May 1745 to advise the Prince not to come over without foreign assistance. He missed the Prince and returned to Scotland. He was certainly captured at sea in December 1745 and put in the Tower, where he was at the end of July 1747. He was ultimately released and exiled, and went to France. *SHS.3.38.*

McDONALD, ALEXANDER, of "Kingsborrow" (Kingsburgh), Skye. Imprisoned July 1746 Fort Augustus; 2.8.1746 Edinburgh Castle, liberated 4.7.1747. Factor to Sir Alexander Macdonald of Sleat. "High Treason and Treasonable practices." Although he had taken no part in the Rising, Kingsburgh was arrested for having shown hospitality to the Prince when, as a fugitive, he took refuge at Kingsburgh House on 29 June. He was arrested shortly afterwards, by order of General Campbell, and accompanied Sir Alexander to Fort Augustus. Thence he was conveyed to Edinburgh Castle, under a cavalry escort. Here he was placed in solitary confinement for a long time and suffered much in his health. The Lord President tried to secure his release in December 1746 but without success. He was liberated on 4 July 1747 upon his preferring a petition wherein he claimed the benefit of the Indemnity. He died 13 Feb 1772, aged 83. *SHS.3.38.*

McDONALD, ALEXANDER, from Culcroich, Glengarry. Imprisoned Edinburgh, discharged. "Confesses that he came up to Dalkeith to join the rebel army, and upon hearing that Sir Alexander McDonald was not there he left them." *SHS.3.40.*

McDONALD, ALEXANDER, Merchant aged 24 from Micklestrath, Ross, Cromarty's Regiment. Imprisoned Inverness June 1746, *Alexander & James, Liberty,* Medway, transported 20.3.1747. *SHS.3.40, MR82.*

McDONALD, ALEXANDER, aged 60, farmer in Glenmoriston, Glengarry's Regiment. Imprisoned Inverness June 1746; prison ship *Dolphin* Tilbury Fort. Transported 1747. *SHS.3.40, MR155, BMHS.30.79.*

McDONALD, ALEXANDER, aged 38, farmer in Glenmoriston, Glengarry's Regiment. Imprisoned inverness June 1746, prison ship *Dolphin* Tilbury Fort. Transported 31 March 1747 from London to Barbados in *Frere. SHS.3.40, MR154, BMHS.30.79.*

McDONALD, ALEXANDER, aged 30, farmer in Glenmoriston, Glengarry's Regiment. Imprisoned Inverness June 1746, prison ship *Dolphin,* Tilbury Fort. Transported 31.3.1747 from London to Barbados in *Frere. SHS.3.40, MR154.*

McDONALD, ALEXANDER, aged 30, farmer in Glenmoriston, home Glen Urquhart, Glengarry's Regiment. Imprisoned Inverness June 1746, prison ship *Dolphin* Tilbury Fort. Transported 31.3.1747 from London to Jamaica in *St George or Carteret,* arriving Jamaica 1747. *SHS.3.40, BMHS.30.79.*

McDONALD, ALEXANDER, aged 46, of Glen Urquhart, Glengarry's Regiment. Imprisoned Inverness June 1746 prison ship *Alexander & James,* Tilbury. Transported 31.3.1747 from London to Jamaica in *St George or Carteret,* arriving Jamaica 1747. *SHS.3.42, MR155, PRO.CO137.58, BMHS.30.79.*

McDONALD, ALEXANDER, aged 30, labourer or cattleherd, Corrimony, Inverness-shire, "Barrisdales" ie Glengarry's Regiment. Imprisoned 4.11.1745 Duddingston; 25.1.1746 Edinburgh Jail, Canongate, 8.8.1746 Carlisle. "Spent 4 nights with the rebels." He must have deserted immediately the Prince's army left Edinburgh. He said he "herded cattle of Grant of Corrimony." Transported 1747. *SHS.3.42*

MacDONALD, ALEXANDER, of Keppoch, killed at Culloden. *SHS.1.294.*

MacDONALD, ALEXANDER, of Glencoe, surrendered, released 11 October 1749. *SHS.1.294.*

MacDONALD or MacDONNELL, ALLAN, the Reverend, from South Uist. Chaplain and Captain, Clanranald's Regiment. Imprisoned South Uist; HMS *Furnace* Tilbury, Southwark. Released 25.5.1747. A kinsman of Clanranald, he went out with the clan regiment as Chaplain and was also Confessor to the Prince, carried arms, and was styled Captain. He accompanied the army to Prestonpans. At Falkirk he rode along the line and gave his blessing before the action. After Culloden he was with the Prince until he reached Scalpa, 2 May 1746. He was captured in South Uist and sent to London in Captain Ferguson's ship the *Furnace,* along with four other priests. He appealed for release, saying that he had no connection with the Rising, and was released by order of the Duke of Newcastle on condition of not returning. He then went to Paris, and in 1748 to Rome. *SHS.3.4.*

McDONALD, ALLAN, aged 36, from Inverness, Cromarty's Regiment. Imprisoned Inverness June 1746, prison ship *Alexander & James,* hospital ship *Liberty & Property,* Tilbury. Transported 31.3.1747 from London to Barbados in *Frere.* Was a soldier in McLeod's company of Loudoun's Regiment, and therefore technically a deserter. *SHS.3.44, MR82, BMHS.30.79.*

McDONALD, ALLAN, of Morar, Lieutenant Colonel, Clanranald's Regiment. Imprisoned Fort William; Fort Augustus, 11.8.1746 Inverness. He was one of the first to meet the Prince in 1745. The Prince came to him in his wanderings for shelter. Albemarle reports his being sent to Inverness. Disposal unknown. *SHS.3.44.*

McDONALD, ALLAN, Barisdale's (Glengarry's) Regiment. Imprisoned Inverness; prison ship *Furnace,* Oct 1746 Tilbury. "Was seen with the rebels at Tain, and heard Barisdale say that he was one of his regiment." "Capt Ferguson reported that he was guilty of many acts of barbarity, and was to be employed by Barisdale to undertake to murder him." He gave evidence against Lord Lovat, and may have been released. Was originally sentenced to be transported but was probably released as an Evidence, 20.3.1747. *SHS.3.44.*

McDONALD, ALLAN, from Moidart, Clanranald's Regiment. Imprisoned 9.6.1746, surrendered to General Campbell; 14.6.1746 Dumbarton. Discharged 29.1.1747. "Brother to

Aeneas McDonald and Donald McDonald of Kinlochmoidart."
According to *Origins* he "fled to France and perished in the
Revolution." *SHS.3.44.*

McDONALD, ALLAN, farmer from Boistill, South Uist, Clanranald's
Regiment. Imprisoned September 1746, prison ship
Pamela, Tilisbury, discharged April 1747. *SHS.3.44.*

McDONALD, ANGUS, farmer at Guilin, Island of Eigg, Inverness-
shire, Clanranald's Regiment. Imprisoned September 1746;
prison ship *Pamela* Tilbury. Transported 20.3.1747 from
Tilbury. *SHS.3.44, BMHS.30.79.*

McDONALD, ANGUS, aged 50, Inverness-shire, Clanranald's
Regiment. Imprisoned Inverness June 1746, prison ship
Pamela Tilbury. Transported 20.3.1747 from Tilbury to
Jamaica in *St George or Carteret*, arriving Jamaica 1747.
SHS.3.44, MR142.

McDONALD, ANGUS, labourer from Ord in Sleat, Clanranald's
Regiment. Imprisoned 4.11.1745 Dalkeith; 15.1.1746
Edinburgh Jail, discharged 9.4.1747. "Says that he was
brought prisoner from the north by the rebels to Dalkeith,
where he was dismissed because he would not join them."
SHS.3.44.

McDONALD, ANGUS, aged 50, labourer from Fort Augustus,
Inverness-shire, Duke of Perth's Regiment. Imprisoned
30.12.1745 Carlisle; York, executed York 1.11.1746.
"Joined the Prentender's son on his first landing, and was in
the rebellion of 1715." Taken at capture of Carlisle. He
pleased guilty at his trial on 2 Oct 1746 and was sentenced
to death. *SHS.3.46.*

McDONALD, ANGUS, tailor at Kirktown of Raasay, Isle of Skye,
McLeod of Raasay's Regiment. Imprisoned Sept 1746
prison ship *Pamela* Tilsbury. Transported from Tilbury
1747. *SHS.3.46, MR185.*

McDONALD, ANGUS, aged 20, farmer from Cromiel, South Uist,
McLeod of Raasay's Regiment. Imprisoned Aug 1746
prison ship *Pamela* Tilsbury. Transported 1747. *SHS.3.46,
MR185.*

McDONALD, ANGUS, labourer from Inverness, "Schien
McDonalds" (Glengarry's) Regiment. Imprisoned
10.11.1745 Dalkeith; 25.1.1745 Edinburgh Jail, 8.8.1746
Carlisle, York Castle. Transported Antigua 8.5.1747.
SHS.3.46, MR155.

McDONALD, ANGUS, aged 64 from "Kilwhinian", Glengarry's
Regiment. Imprisoned Inverness June 1746, prison ship

Jane of Alloway. No further reference to him. He may have died. *SHS.3.46.*

McDONALD, ANGUS, aged 40, Glengarry's Regiment. Imprisoned 21.9.1745 Prestonpans; 22.9.1745 Edinburgh Royal Infirmary, Canongate, 8.8.1746 Carlisle. Wounded at Prestonpans; gunshot of haunch. *SHS.3.46.*

McDONALD, ANGUS, aged 50, from Rannoch, Keppoch's Regiment. Imprisoned 1.2.1746 Torwood; 7.2.1746 Stirling Castle; 13.2.1746 Lieth Edinburgh, 8.8.1746 Carlisle, York Castle. Transported 1747. "Pressed by the Highlanders." *SHS.3.46, MR164.*

McDONALD or MacDONELL of Barisdale, ARCHIBALD, from Knoydart. Known as Old Barisdale." Uncle of John McDonald of Glengarry and brother of Angus McDonald of Scotus. He paid his respects to the Prince at Glenfinnan but took no personal part in the Rising. In May 1746, his house was burnt down by Cumberland's orders and he was himself taken prisoner and placed in a warship. He was released soon afterwards. He died 1752. *SHS.3.48.*

McDONALD or MacDONELL of Barisdale, ARCHIBALD, youngest, Major, Glengarry's Regiment. Imprisoned June 1746 Fort Augustus, released conditionally; 13.3.1749 arrested but released, 18.7.1753 Edinburgh Castle, released 29.3.1762. Known as "youngest Barisdale." Son of Coll MacDonell and grandson of Archibald Macdonell of Barisdale, he joined the Prince at the age of 20. He was captured along with his father (Coll Macdonell), released, and was then captured by the Jacobites under suspicion of treachery, and was sent over in the same ship as the Prince to France, where he was kept for a year. He returned to Scotland, and in 1749 was again arrested by Government, but was released. Again, on 18 June 1753, he was arrested, tried and sentenced to death on 22 March 1754 by the Lords of Justiciary. He was however reprieved, but kept as a prisoner until 29 March 1762, when he was finally released. He then took the oath of fealty to the Government and was given a commission in the "Queen's Own Royal Highlanders." He died at Barisdale in 1787. *SHS.3.48, SHS.1.294.*

McDONALD, ARCHIBALD, aged 42, farmer in Glenmoriston, Glengarry's Regiment. Imprisoned Inverness June 1746, prison ship *Wallsgrave*, Tilbury Fort. Transported 31.3.1747. *SHS.3.48, MR164, BMHS.30.79.*

McDONALD, ARCHIBALD, aged 25, servant to farmer in Kilcreich, Inverness, McLachlan's Regiment. Imprisoned Inverness; Tilbury Fort. Transported 20.3.1747 from Tilbury. *SHS.3.48.*

McDONALD, ARCHIBALD, aged 54, from Inverness, Cromarty's Regiment. Imprisoned Inverness, June 1746 prison ship *Alexander & James*. Transported from Liverpool to Virginia in *Johnson*, died 4 June 1747 at sea. *SHS.1.187, SHS.3.48, MR155, PRO.T1.328.*

McDONALD, ARCHIBALD, aged 45, labourer from Inverness-shire, Keppoch's Regiment. Imprisoned 4.11.1745 Duddingston; Edinburgh Castle, 15.1.1746 Edinburgh Jail, Carlisle. Common highlander, deserted from the Prince's Army. *SHS.3.48.*

McDONALD, ARCHIBALD, from Clenaig, Lochaber, "an officer in Lochiel's" Regiment. Imprisoned 13.11.1745 Dalkeith; 22.11.1745 Edinburgh Jail, 8.8.1746 Carlisle. His fate is unknown. *SHS.3.50.*

McDONALD, ARCHIBALD, aged 27, from Mull, McLachlan's Regiment. Imprisoned Inverness June 1746; prison ship *Jane of Alloway*". No further reference to him. *SHS.3.50.*

McDONALD or MacDONNELL, COLL, younger of Barisdale, aged 47. Commanded Glengarry's Regiment. Imprisoned 10.6.1746 Fort Augustus, released conditionally; re-arrested Feb 1749, Edinburgh Castle. Died in Edinburgh prison, 1 June 1750. "Collin Roy," red Colin. "Young Barisdale." Was eldest son of Archibald Macdonell, the "Old Barisdale." He joined the Prince at Aberchalder on 27.8.1745 at the head of Glengarry's men from Knoydart, and served throughout the campaign and fought at Falkirk but missed Culloden, as he was in Ross-shire. He was captured in June 1746 along with his son Archibald, and was taken to Fort Augustus, but was given a ten days' protection on condition of giving certain information to the Government. It was also said that he had engaged to apprehend the Prince and hand him over to the Government. For this he was seized by the Jacobites, who succeeded in getting him across to France and keeping him a prisoner in St Malo for over two years. Family tradition states that he deliberately misled the authorities and that his capture by his own side was due to an old quarrel with the Camerons over the theft of cattle. Meanwhile the Government excluded him from the Act of Indemnity in 1747. When he returned home in Feb

1749 he was again arrested by Government, and confined in Edinburgh Castle without trial until his death, June 1750. *SHS.1.187, SHS.3.50.*

McDONALD, COLL, Glengarry's Regiment, Badivochal, Elgin. Imprisoned Carlisle; York Castle. Drowned at Liverpool when going on board a ship for transportation, March 1747. "Carried arms. Prisoner." *SHS.1.187, SHS.3.50.*

McDONALD, DANIEL, born 1728, labourer from Lettochbeag, Kinloch, Inverness-shire. Imprisoned 30.12.1745 Carlisle; Chester Castle. Transported 5 May 1747, from Liverpool to Leeward Islands, in *Veteran*, arriving Martinique June 1747. *SHS.3.52, PRO.SP36.102.*

McDONALD, DONALD, Inverness-shire, Colonel and ADC to the Prince. Imprisoned Nov 1745, Lesmahagow; 12.11.1745 Edinburgh Castle, 15.1.1746 Edinburgh Tolbooth, 8.8.1746 Carlisle. Executed Carlisle 18.10.1746. Kinlochmoidart was one of the first to join the Prince when he landed in Scotland. He was at once sent to summon the Duke of Perth, Lochiel, and John Murray of Broughton. He was employed by the Prince as an emissary, and in this capacity was sent to Lord Lovat. He was made a Colonel and, according to a statement by his brother Aeneas Macdonald, "was to have been made a baronet and peer of Scotland." He was caught at Lesmahagow in Nov 1745 while returning from an unsuccessful mission to Sir Alexander McDonald of Sleat and McLeod. When captured he was found to have in his possession a letter from the Prince's Securetary, Murray, telling him to spread the report that the McLeods and Sir Alexander McDonald were on the march "notwithstanding you may have received contrary information." This letter was dated Holyrood, 27 Oct 1745. He was sent to Carlisle and tried and convicted. After his execution his head was affixed to the Scots Gate, Carlisle, where it remained for many years. His house too was burnt down. *SHS.3.52.*

McDONALD or MacDONELL of Tiendrish (Tirnadrish), DONALD, Inverness-shire, Major, Keppoch's Regiment. Imprisoned 17.1.1746 Battle of Falkirk; Carlisle. Executed 18.10.1746. Son of Ronald Mor of Tir-na-Dris, second son of McDonald of Keppoch. He was the first to draw blood in the Jacobite cause, as it was he, with a few men, who attacked two companies of Guise's regiment near Fort William on 14 Aug 1745, and captured Captains Swetenham and John Scott and killed two or three men. He added to his offence on this occasion by capturing Capt Scott's horse and presenting it to the Prince at Glenfinnan. At the battle of Falkirk he mistook some English troops in the dusk for men of Lord John Drummond, and was captured and narrowly escapted being shot on the spot. When in Carlisle Castle he wrote cheerfully to his friends, notably when he sent a message to a lady "that notwithstanding of my irons I could dance a Highland reel with her." *SHS.3.52.*

McDONALD, DONALD, from Argyllshire, Stewart of "Innerheils" (Invernahyle). Imprisoned 21.9.1745 Prestonpans; 22.9.1745 Edinburgh Royal Infirmary, 5.5.1746 Canongate, 8.8.1746 Carlisle. Executed Brampton 24.10.1746. Wounded at Prestonpans; bullet wound through leg. *SHS.3.54.*

McDONALD or McDONELL, DONALD (or Daniel or David), aged 25 from Inverness-shire, Captain, Keppoch's Regiment. Imprisoned 30.12.1745 Carlisle; London. Executed Kennington Common 22.8.1746. Captured at capitulation of Carlisle. He was said at his trial in London to be nephew of James Nicolson, a fellow-prisoner. He pleaded guilty and begged for mercy, but was hanged "in highland dress." *SHS.3.54.*

McDONALD, DONALD, of Benbecula, Captain, Morven, Argyll, Clanranald's Regiment. Imprisoned Edinburgh Castle, pardoned 28.10.1748. Second son of Ranald McDonald of Clanranald, he served in the regiment of his brother Ranald, "young Clanranald." After Culloden he was skulking for some time but was captured and sent to Edinburgh Castle, from which he was discharged without trial in Oct 1748, having received an unconditional pardon. In 1756 he joined the Fraser Highlanders, under the Master of Lovat, and served with Wolfe at Quebec. He was subsequently killed in a later action. *SHS.3.54.*

McDONALD, DONALD, from Morven, Argyll, farmer, Gruilin, Eigg, Clanranald's Regiment. Imprisoned Sept 1746, prison ship *Pamela*, Tilbury, released 11.6.1747. This may have been the Donald McDonald who turned King's Evidence and was confined in the house of Dick the messenger, and was released on 11 June 1747. *SHS.3.54.*

McDONALD, DONALD, farmer at Fivepenny, Eigg, Morven, Argyll, Clanranald's Regiment. Imprisoned Sept 1746 prison ship *Pamela* Tilbury. "Taken up on suspicion but never was in the Rebellion." Nevertheless he was transported 19.3.1747 from London to Jamaica, in *St George or Carteret*, arriving Jamaica 1747. *SHS.3.54, BMHS.30.79.*

McDONALD, DONALD, aged 56, farmer at Clatil in Eigg, from Isle of Uist, Sergeant, Clanranald's Regiment. Imprisoned Sept 1746, prison ship *Pamela* Tilbury. Transported 31.3.1747 from London to Jamaica in *St George or Carteret*, arriving Jamaica 1747. This was perhaps brother of Ronald McDonald, Bailie of Benbecula. *SHS.3.56, PRO.CO137.58, MR141, BMHS.30.79.*

McDONALD, DONALD, aged 50, farmer in Glen Urquhart, Glengarry's Regiment. Imprisoned Inverness June 1746, prison ship *Dolphin* Tilbury Fort. Transported 31.3.1747 from London to Jamaica in *St George or Carteret*, arriving Jamaica 1747. *SHS.3.56, BMHS.30.79.*

McDONALD, DONALD, aged 25, from Glen Urquhart, Glengarry's Regiment. Imprisoned Inverness June 1746, prison ship *Thane of Fife* Tilbury. Transported 20.3.1747 from Tilbury to Jamaica in *St George or Carteret*, arriving Jamaica 1747. *SHS.3.56, MR155, PRO.CO137.58, BMHS.30.79.*

McDONALD, DONALD, from Inverness-shire, Glengarry's Regiment. Imprisoned Inverness June 1746, prison ship *Thane of Fife* Tilbury. Transported 20.3.1747 (or 31.3.1747 from London to Barbados, in *Frere*. *SHS.3.56.*

McDONALD, DONALD, aged 22, labourer from Inverness, Glengarry's Regiment. Imprisoned Carlisle; Lancaster Castle, York Castle. Transported Antigua 8.5.1747 from Liverpool in *Veteran*, arriving Martinique June 1747. *SHS.3.56, MR156, PRO.SP36.102.*

McDONALD, DONALD, aged 19, labourer from Inverness, Glengarry's Regiment. Imprisoned Carlisle; York Castle. Acquitted Sept 1746. Was tried at Carlisle 19/26 Sept 1746 and acquitted. *SHS.3.56.*

McDONALD, DONALD, aged 22, labourer from Inverness, Lovat's Regiment. Imprisoned Inverness June 1746, prison ship *Wallsgrave*, Tilbury. Transported 5 May 1747 from Liverpool to Leeward Islands in *Veteran*, arriving Martinique June 1747. *SHS.3.56, MR156, PRO.SP36.102.*

MacDONALD, DONALD, of Lochgarry, escaped *SHS.1.294*

MacDONALD, DONALD, son of Ranald Macdonald of Clanranald, captured, released without trial. *SHS.1.294.*

McDONALD, DOUGAL, aged 50, from Glenmoriston, Glengarry's Regiment. Imprisoned inverness June 1746, prison ship

Dolphin. No further reference to him. May have died. *SHS.3.58.*

McDONALD, DUNCAN, aged 41, Cromarty's Regiment. Imprisoned Inverness, Tilbury Fort. Discharged. Turned King's Evidence against Lieutenant Hector McKenzie. *SHS.3.58.*

McDONALD, DUNCAN, aged 21, servant from Inverness, Lovat's Regiment. Imprisoned Inverness June 1746, prison ship *Alexander & James,* hospital ship *Liberty & Prosperity,* Medway. Transported 31.3.1747 from London to Barbados in *Frere.* Servant to brother of Fraser of Culdutal. *SHS.3.58, MR118.*

McDONALD, DUNCAN, aged 45, farmer in Glenmoriston, Glengarry's Regiment. Imprisoned Inverness June 1746, prison ship *Dolphin* Tilbury Fort. Transported 31.3.1747 from London to Barbados in *Frere.* *SHS.3.58, MR156, BMHS.30.79.*

McDONALD, DUNCAN, aged 40, farmer in Glen Urquhart, Glengarry's Regiment. Imprisoned Inverness June 1746, prison ship *Wallsgrave,* Tilbury, Tilbury Fort. Subsequent history not traced. *SHS.3.58.*

McDONALD, EWEN, Glengarry's Regiment. Imprisoned Inverness, Tilbury Fort. Transported from Tilbury Fort. *SHS.3.58, MR156.*

McDONALD, FLORA, born 1722, from Isle of Skye. Imprisoned July 1746 Skye; Dunstaffnage Castle, HMS *Furnace;* HMS *Brigewater (Commodore Thomas Smith),* 28.11.1746 HMS *Royal Sovereign, the Nore;* 6.12.1746 London, Mr Dick the Messenger's House. Released July 1747. Her father died in her infancy, and she was step-daughter to Hugh Macdonald of Armadale. She was sister of Angus Macdonald of Milton, one of the cadets of Macdonald of Clanranald, and was adopted by Lady Clanranald, chief of the clan. She met the Prince at Ormaclett in South Uist, and arranged to help him to get across to Skye, which they did on 29 June. She accompanied him to Portree, and there left him on 1 July. A few days later she was captured near Sleat and placed in the Furnace where, owing to the presence on board of General Campbell, she was well treated. From the beginning of September to 7 November she was in HMS *Bridgewater* in Leith harbour, and was allowed to meet her friends, and to be entertained by them. On 28 November she was placed in the *Royal Sovereign* at the Nore, and thence transferred on 6 December to London to the house of a messenger, Mr Dick, where there were several other Jacobite prisoners. She was released in July 1747, and in 1750 she married Allan, son of Alexander Macdonald of Kingsburgh. In 1775 they emigrated to North Carolina, and when the War of Independence broke out he became a Brigadier-General, and was made prisoner. She returned home in 1779, and her husband ultimately rejoined her at Kingsburgh. She died 5 March 1790. *SHS.1.215, SHS.3.58.*

McDONALD, GEORGE (or GORIE), "Common highlander." "Carrying baggage." Imprisoned on suspicion 4.11.1745 Duddingston; Edinburgh Castle, 15.1.1746 Edinburgh Jail. Discharged. *SHS.3.60.*

McDONALD, or MACDONALD, HUGH, Bishop. Imprisoned July 1755 Edinburgh Castle; Duns. Sentenced to be banished, but finally released. Son of Alexander Macdonald of Morar. He was Catholic Bishop of Diana and Vicar-Apostolic of the Highlands. When the Prince arrived in Scotland he went to him and begged him to go back; and when the Standard was raised at Glenfinnan he blessed it. After Culloden he was with Lord Lovat in his hiding place in Morar, but when Lovat was captured the Bishop escaped and went to France in September 1746. He returned in 1749 to Scotland, but was arrested in July 1755 and released on bail and ordered to stay at Duns. In February 1756 he was sentenced by the high Court to perpetual banishment, but the sentence was not enforced, and he remained in Scotland until his death in 1773. *SHS.3.60.*

McDONALD, HUGH, aged 30, from Glenmoriston, Glengarry's Regiment. Imprisoned Inverness June 1746, prison ship *Dolphin.* Transported 1747. *SHS.3.60, MR156.*

McDONALD, HUGH, aged 35, from Glen Urquhart, Glengarry's Regiment. Imprisoned Inverness June 1746, prison ship *Dolphin.* Nothing more is known of him. *SHS.3.60.*

McDONALD, HUGH, aged 22, labourer from Tarbert, Canna, "Fairbacks" Regiment. Imprisoned 6.11.1745 Duddingston; 25.1.1746 Edinburgh Jail. Discharged. "Says that he came to Edinburgh as a servant to John McLachlan, drover, while the rebels were there, and having fallen sick at Edinburgh, was left at a village in the neighbourhood along with some sick rebels. *SHS.3.62.*

McDONALD, HUGH, aged 13, from Arisaig. Imprisoned York Castle; Lincoln Castle. Transported 22.4.1747 (5.5.1747?) from Liverpool to Leeward Islands in *Veteran*, arriving Martinique June 1747. *SHS.3.62, PRO.SP36.102.*

McDONALD, JAMES, from Canna. Imprisoned London May 1746, released 25.5.1747. Uncle of Alexander of Glenaladale. "Bailie of Canna." General Campbell lifted his cattle and sent him a prisoner to London "where he continued upwards of twelve months, notwithstanding of loudoun's protection." *SHS.3.62.*

McDONALD, JAMES, aged 47, farmer at Guilin, Island of Eigg, Clanranald's Regiment. Imprisoned Sept 1746 prison ship *Pamela*, Tilbury. Transported 31.3.1747 from London to Jamaica, in *St George or Carteret*, arriving Jamaica 1747. He was probably the factor of Clanranald in Canna. Stated also to be still in Tilbury Fort in April 1747. *SHS.3.62, MR142, PRO.CO137.58, BMHS.30.79.*

McDONALD, JAMES, tacksman of Gerrihellie, South Uist. Youngest son of Alexander the Bard of the Dalelea family. Visited the Prince when in hiding in Coradale. Arrested on suspicion, but released for lack of evidence. *SHS.3.62.*

McDONALD, JAMES, from Moidart, Clanranald's Regiment. Imprisoned Culloden, escaped. Brother to Kinlochmoidart. Was captured at Culloden but escaped. He was excepted from the General Pardon and is supposed to have gone to America. *SHS.3.62.*

McDONALD, JAMES, aged 49, farmer in Glenmoriston, Glen Urquhart, Glengarry's Regiment. Imprisoned Inverness June 1746, prison ship *Dolphin*, Tilbury Fort. Transported 20.3.1747 from Tilbury to Jamaica in *St George or Carteret*, arriving Jamaica 1747. *SHS.3.64.*

McDONALD or McDONELL of Glengarry, JOHN, Colonel and Chief of Glengarry. Imprisoned 21.8.1746, surrendered, Fort Augustus; 21.8.1746 Edinburgh Castle. Released 11.10.1749. "Witnesses saw him in arms marching at the head of a body of rebels, and that he was called their Colonel, and was wearing a white cockade." "Subsisted himself" while imprisoned in Edinburgh Castle. In spite of the evidence Glengarry did not himself go out, but actually joined Cope at Crieff soon after the Prince landed. His second son, Angus, commanded the clan and was killed at Falkirk accidentally. Shortly after Culloden the old chief was imprisoned, and was not released until October 1749. He was specially excepted from the Act of Pardon of June 1747. Writing to Newcastle about him on 1 September 1746, Albemarle said "he may be wrongfully accused as he showed a remarkable inclination to be useful to the King's troops at Fort Augustus, and when he was employed by me." He appealed for release under the Act of 1701 regarding wrongous imprisonment, and was discharged on 11 October 1749. *SHS.3.64.*

McDONALD, JOHN, Dr, surgeon in Moidart, brother of Kinlochmoidart, who served as a Captain in Clanranald's regiment. He was captured in June 1746, imprisoned in Eigg; HMS *Furnace (Captain Ferguson)*, Sept 1746 prison ship *Pamela*, Tilbury, House of Dick the Messenger in London. He was kept in the *Pamela*, without trial, until the end of the year, and was then transferred to the house of Dick the Messenger. He was released 11 June 1747 for want of evidence, and having been "out" in the "15 with his father, must be regarded as fortunate. *SHS.1.218, SHS.3.64.*

McDONALD, JOHN, aged 40, farmer at Galmistal, Eigg. Morar, Inverness. Clanranald's Regiment. Imprisoned Sept 1746 prison ship *Pamela*, Tilbury. Transported 20.3.1747. *SHS.3.66, MR142.*

McDONALD, JOHN, aged 29, farmer at Clatich, Island of Eigg, Clanranald's Regiment. Imprisoned prison ship *Pamela*, Tilbury, released 11.6.1747. Sent for trial. He does not appear, however, to have been tried, and was put in the house of Dick the messenger. This perhaps suggests that he turned King's Evidence. There he stayed until June 1747, when he was released. *SHS.3.66.*

McDONALD, JOHN, aged 36, farmer at Howlin in Eigg, Clanranald's Regiment. Imprisoned June 1746 prison ship *Pamela*, Tilbury. Transported 20.3.1747 from Tilbury. *SHS.3.66, MR142.*

McDONALD, JOHN, aged 58, farmer in Fivepenny, Eigg, Inverness-shire, Clanranald's Regiment. Imprisoned June 1746, prison ship *Pamela*, Tilbury. Transported 30.3.1747 from London to Barbados, in Frere. *SHS.3.66, MR142.*

McDONALD, JOHN, aged 36, farmer at Glenistill, Eigg, Clanranald's Regiment. Imprisoned June 1746, prison ship *Pamela*, Tilbury. Transported 20.3.1747 from Tilbury. *SHS.3.66, MR142.*

McDONALD, JOHN, labourer from Ord of Sleat, Clanranald's Regiment. Imprisoned 4.11.1745 Dalkeith; 25.1.1746 Edinburgh Jail. Discharged 17.4.1747. "Says he was brought a prisoner to Edinburgh by some of the rebels, and was dismissed by them at Dalkeith, having refused to join them." *SHS.3.66.*

McDONALD, (alias McIllinian), JOHN, from Tiree, McLean of Drimnin's Regiment. Imprisoned August 1746 Tiree; Dumbarton Castle, 4.2.1747 Glasgow. Discharged 15.7.1747. "Says he was with rebels two or three days before Culloden." As a matter of fact he attended McLean of Drimnin when recruiting men in the island. *SHS.3.66.*

McDONALD, JOHN, from Gellevie, Badenoch, Keppoch's Regiment. Imprisoned Edinburgh, discharged. "Confesses that he marched with the rebels to Kelso attending the baggage belonging to Donald McDonald, brother to Keppoch, and there deserted. *SHS.3.66.*

McDONALD, JOHN (alias Campbell), from Glenmoriston. Imprisoned Nov 1746 Inverness, released. One of the famous eight men of Glenmoriston who, having served in the Jacobite army (*Cameron Lees*, Inverness, 191), were living the life of outlaws, and terrorised the Government troops about Fort Augustus. With them the Prince stayed several days in Aug 1746. Distressed at the Princes' mean clothing they shot some servants carrying baggage for officers at the barracks in order that he might be better clad. They did not leave until he got back to Loch Arkaig. Chisholm of Strathglass, on whose land the incident of the shooting had taken place, undertook to make the men prisoners, and in Nov 1746 John McDonald was captured and taken to inverness. As, however, there was no proof against him he was released under the Indemnity, and emigrated to America. *SHS.3.68.*

McDONALD, JOHN, labourer from Badenoch, Keppoch's Regiment. Imprisoned 4.11.1745 Duddingston; 25.1.1746 Edinburgh Tolbooth, 8.8.1746 Carlisle. Transported 19.3.1747. *SHS.3.68, MR164.*

McDONALD, JOHN, from Achallander, Glen Orchy, Argyll, Kepploch's Regiment. Imprisoned Harbour (?Larbert) bridge near Falkirk; 5.2.1746 Edinburgh Jail. Discharged. "Says he was pressed by one Alexander McNab to serve him as baggage man in the rebel army." *SHS.3.68.*

McDONALD, JOHN, labourer, from Badenoch, Inverness-shire, Keppoch's Regiment. Imprisoned 13.1.1746 Linlithgow; 20.1.1746 Leith, 7.2.1746 Edinburgh, 8.8.1746 Carlisle. Transported 19.3.1747. *SHS.3.68, MR164.*

McDONALD, JOHN, from Inverness. Imprisoned 28.5.1746 from Town Guard at Edinburgh Castle; 17.6.1746 Edinburgh Jail, Canongate Jail. Released under General Pardon, 1747. Edinburgh Town Guard. "Journeyman mason. Servant to Charles Mack, mason in Edinburgh." On suspicion. "Denies that he was concerned with the rebellion." *SHS.3.68.*

McDONALD, (or McDonough) JOHN, husbandman aged 14, from Isle of Barra, Argyllshire. Imprisoned Inverness June 1746, prison ship *James & Mary*, Medway. Transported 20.3.1747. "Servant to Sweeny, a French officer." *SHS.3.70, MR164.*

McDONALD, JOHN, aged 30, servant to Daniel Grant in Glenmoriston, Glengarry's Regiment. Imprisoned Inverness June 1746, prison ship *Dolphin*, Tilbury Fort. Died June 1746. *SHS.3.70.*

McDONALD, JOHN, aged 60, farmer in Glenmoriston, Glengarry's Regiment. Imprisoned Inverness June 1746, prison ship *Dolphin*, Tilbury Fort. Transported 31.3.1747 from London to Barbados in *Frere*. *SHS.3.70, MR156, BMHS.30.79.*

McDONALD, JOHN, aged 56 (50?), tailor near Sir Alexander McDonald, Isle of Skye, Glengarry's Regiment. Imprisoned on "suspicion only," Inverness June 1746, prison ship *Wallsgrave*, Tilbury, Tilbury Fort. Transported 31.3.1747 from London to Jamaica, on *St George or Carteret*, arriving Jamaica 1747. *SHS.3.70, MR157, PRO.CO137.58, BMHS.30.79.*

McDONALD, JOHN, aged 30, farmer in Glen Urquhart, Glengarry's Regiment. Imprisoned Inverness June 1746, prison ship *Dolphin*, Tilbury Fort. Transported 20.3.1747 from Tilbury to Jamaica in *St George or Carteret*, arriving Jamaica 1747. *SHS.3.70, MR156, PRO.CO137.58, BMHS.30.80.*

McDONALD, JOHN, aged 20, from Glengarry. Herded cattle near Doune. Glengarry's Regiment. Imprisoned Inverness, Tilbury Fort. Transported 20.3.1747. *SHS.3.70, MR156, BMHS.30.80.*

McDONALD, JOHN, aged 20, tailor, Inverness, Glengarry's Regiment. Imprisoned Inverness, hospital ship *Liberty*. Transported 31.3.1747 from London to Jamaica on *St*

George or Carteret, arriving Jamaica 1747. *SHS.3.70, MR156, PRO.CO137.58, BMHS.30.79.*

McDONALD, JOHN, aged 40, cowherd, Dongin, Glengarry, Inverness-shire, Glengarry's Regiment. Imprisoned Inverness June 1746, prison ship *Thane of Fife*, Sept 1746 prison ship *Pamela*, Tilbury. Transported 20.3.1747 from Tilbury to Jamaica in *St George or Carteret*, arriving Jamaica 1747. *SHS.3.70, MR156, PRO.CO137.58, BMHS.30.80.*

McDONALD, JOHN, aged 56, from Redorach, Elgin District, Glengarry's Regiment. Imprisoned Inverness June 1746, prison ship *Dolphin*, Tilbury Fort. Transported 20.3.1747 from Tilbury. "Forced to carry arms. Has submitted himself prisoner." *SHS.3.70, MR157.*

McDONALD, JOHN, aged 40, labourer on the land of the Laird of Scotus, Inverness-shire, Glengarry's Regiment. Imprisoned Inverness June 1746, prison ship *Alexander & James*, hospital ship *Liberty & Property*, Medway. Transported 31.3.1747 from London to Jamaica, in *St George or Carteret*, arriving Jamaica 1747. *SHS.3.72, MR157, PRO.CO137.58, BMHS.30.79.*

McDONALD, JOHN, aged 60, from Inverness. Imprisoned Inverness, June 1746 prison ship *Thane of Fife*. "Servant to young Chisholm." Nothing more is known of him. *SHS.3.72*

McDONALD, JOHN, *Alexander & James*. Died 19.5.1746. *SHS.3.72.*

McDONALD, JOHN, Glengarry's Regiment, died at Tilbury, June 1746. *SHS.1.187.*

McDONALD, JOHN, Glengarry's Regiment, died at sea on prison ship *Alexander & James*, 19 May 1746. *SHS.1.187.*

McDONALD, JOHN BANE, aged 22 from Benbecula. Imprisoned Lancaster Castle. Transported Antigua 8.5.1747. "Servant to Benbecula." "Evidence against his master." *SHS.3.72.*

McDONALD, KENNETH Imprisoned Oct 1746 London, released 10.6.1747. In June 1747 was in the custody of Dick, the messenger. "Evidence against McKinnon and others." *SHS.3.72.*

McDONALD, LACHLAN, from Dremisdale, South Uist. Released. Bailie of South Uist. Son of "Alexander the Bard" of the Dalelea family. Arrested on suspicion of assisting the Prince to escape. Released for want of evidence. *SHS.3.72*

McDONALD, of Clanranald, Lady MARGARET. Imprisoned July 1746 Tilbury, London, in messenger's house. Liberated on bail 4.7.1747. Daughter of William Macleod of Luskintyre. Wife of Ranald McDonald of Clanranald. This was the lady who met and entertained the Prince on 27 June 1746 at Rossinish. She was taken prisoner shortly afterwards, and sent to London. General Campbell reported that "she had not only been very zealous herself in serving the Young Pretender while on the Long Island but has brought her husband and several others into the same scrape." The Privy Council on 31 March decided to release her on bail to appear before the Court of Justiciary in Edinburgh. *SHS.3.72.*

McDONALD, MARGARET, aged 21, from Inverness. Imprisoned Inverness, prison ship *Thane of Fife*, prison ship *James & Mary*, Medway. Transported 1747. Taken up at Inverness for endeavouring to delude the King's men to desert. *SHS.1.216, SHS.3.72.*

McDONALD, MARGARET, released *SHS.1.216.*

McDONALD, MARY, aged 35, from Inverness. Imprisoned in Lancaster Castle. Transported 1747. *SHS.1.216, SHS.3.74.*

McDONALD, OWEN, Glengarry's Regiment. Imprisoned Inverness,Tilbury. Transported 20.3.1747. *SHS.3.74, MR157, BMHS.30.80.*

McDONALD, OWEN, aged 40, farmer in Glen Urquhart, Glengarry's Regiment. Imprisoned Inverness, Tilbury Fort. Transported 31.3.1747 from London to Barbados on *Frere*. *SHS.3.74, MR157, BMHS.30.80.*

McDONALD, PATRICK, Glengarry's Regiment. Imprisoned York Castle, Chester Castle. Released 3.8.1747. "Taken in actual rebellion." *SHS.3.74.*

McDONALD, PETER, aged 17. Imprisoned York Castle. Reprieved and pardoned on condition of enlistment 22.7.1748. Pleaded guilty at his trial, 2 Oct 1746, and was sentenced to death, but reprieved. *SHS.3.74.*

McDONALD, RANALD, Clanranald's Regiment. Imprisoned ?Fort William, Fort Augustus, 11.8.1746 Inverness. Transported. This may be the man referred to by Lord Albemarle. *SHS.3.74.*

McDONALD, of Clanranald, RANALD, senior, South Uist. Imprisoned Tilbury, 1.11.1746 London (in a messenger's house). Liberated 4.7.1747. He took no part in the Rising, but on two occasions after Culloden he visited the fugitive Prince. He was included in the Bill of Attainder of June

1746, and was apprehended on the charge of having helped the Prince to escape. His wife was taken at the same time. On 25 May 1747 the Privy Council decided that he should be prosecuted in Scotland, but he appears to have been released under the General Pardon. *SHS.3.74.*

McDONALD, of Clanranald, RANALD, younger, Lieutenant Colonel, Clanranald's Regiment. Imprisoned 1752 London (messenger's house). Released April 1754. Eldest son of Ranald McDonald of Clanranald; raised his father's clan shortly after the Prince landed. He commanded the regiment and served through the campaign, being badly wounded at Culloden. He was in hiding for eighteen months in Moidart, during which period he got married. He then went to France and obtained military employment there. He returned in June 1752, apparently thinking there was no attainder in operation. He was however imprisoned and kept in a messenger's house in London until April 1754, when he was released. It was stated that he hoped "to evade the effect of his attainder, on account of a misnomer in the Act of Pariament," and was arrested. *SHS.3.76.*

MacDONALD, RANALD, of Belfinlay, aged 20, Captain, Clanranald's Regiment. Imprisoned 17.4.1746 Inverness. Released 1747. He was 18 years old when he joined the army. A cadet of the Clanranald's. He was wounded in the legs at Culloden and was stripped of his clothes. He was on the point of being shot as he lay when a Lieutenant Hamilton saved his life. He was taken to Inverness and kept there until the Indemnity, when he was released. He died in September 1749. *SHS.3.76.*

McDONALD, RANALD, aged 50, from Benbecula, Clanranald's Regiment. Imprisoned Oct 1746 London (Tilbury). "Bailie of Benbecula. Gentleman." He was ordered to be transported, but was still in Tilbury Fort in April 1747. Against his name appears "material evidence against Clanranald, his lady, Boisdale." Probably discharged. *SHS.3.76.*

McDONALD (or MacEachain), RANALD, of Garifleuch, Coradale, South Uist. Imprisoned Tilbury, London. Released under General Pardon, 1747. Brother of Neil Macdonald or MacEachain, the Prince's guide and attendant in the Hebrides. Ranald took the Prince into his house in Coradale, and he was there until 5 June. Ranald was taken prisoner shortly after and sent to London. This is probably the man who was sent to messenger Munie's house to look after Lady Clanranald when she went mad. On 25 May 1747 the Privy Council decided that he should enter into recognisance to appear before the Court of Justiciary in Edinburgh; but he was released under the General Indemnity in July 1747. *SHS.3.76.*

McDONALD, RANALD or RONALD, from Morven, Argyll, farmer at Grinlin, Eigg, Clanranald's Regiment. Imprisoned Sept 1746, prison ship *Pamela*, Tilbury. Transported 31.3.1747. *SHS.3.76, MR143, BMHS.30.80.*

McDONALD, RANALD or RONALD, Inverness-shire, Clanranald's Regiment. Imprisoned 4.11.1745 Duddingston; Edinburgh Castle, 15.1.1746 Edinburgh Tolbooth, 8.8.1746 Carlisle. Executed at Brampton 21.10.1746. "A common highlander." On suspicion. He must have deserted from the Prince's army when it left Edinburgh. *SHS.3.76.*

McDONALD, RODERICK (RORY), released 10.6.1747. This was probably the Rory who was one of the Prince's boatmen on his escape from the mainland to the Isles. His movements are unknown until his name appears as in the custody of Dick the messenger in June 1747. This looks as if he had turned King's Evidence. *SHS.3.78.*

McDONALD, RODERICK, labourer from Laggie of Glengarry, Inverness-shire, Glengarry's Regiment. Imprisoned 4.11.1745, Duddingston; Edinburgh Castle, 25.1.1746 Edinburgh Jail. Discharged. "Says he was brought a prisoner by the rebels to Dalkeith where he deserted from them." *SHS.3.78.*

McDONALD, RODERICK or ROGER, aged 22, "husbandry at Sandvegg, Eigg," Morven, Argyll, Clanranald's Regiment. Imprisoned Sept 1746, prison ship *Pamela*, Tilbury. Transported 31.3.1747 from London to Jamaica, in *St George or Carteret*, arriving Jamaica 1747. *SHS.3.78, BMHS.30.80.*

McDONALD, RODERICK or ROGER, farmer at Kirktown, Island of Eigg, Clanranald's Regiment. Imprisoned Inverness Sept 1746, prison ship *Pamela*, Tilbury. Transported 31.3.1747 from London to Barbados in *Frere*. *SHS.3.78, MR143, BMHS.30.80.*

McDONALD, SWEEN, aged 18, Beggar boy from Inverness, Lord Lovat's Regiment. Imprisoned Inverness June 1746, prison ship *Jane of Alloway*, Tilbury Fort. Transported 31.3.1747

from London to Barbados in *Frere*. On suspicion.
SHS.3.78, MR118, BMHS.30.80.
McDONALD, WILLIAM, aged 35, farmer in Glen Urquhart, Inverness-shire, Glengarry's Regiment. Imprisoned Inverness, June 1746 prison ship *Dolphin*, Tilbury Fort. Transported 31.3.1747. *SHS.3.78, BMHS.30.80.*
McDONALD, WILLIAM, aged 50, farmer in Glenmoriston, org. Glen Urquhart, Glengarry's Regiment. Imprisoned Inverness, Tilbury Fort. Transported 31.3.1747 from London to Jamaica in *St George or Carteret*, arriving Jamaica 1747. *SHS.3.78, MR157, PRO.CO137.58, BMHS.30.80.*
McDONALD, WILLIAM, aged 32 (35?), from Glenmoriston, Glengarry's Regiment. Imprisoned Inverness, June 1746 prison ship *Dolphin*. *SHS.3.78, BMHS.30.80.*
McDONALD, WILLIAM, from Inverness-shire, Keppoch's Regiment. Imprisoned 4.11.1745 Duddingston, Edinburgh Castle, 15.1.1746 Edinburgh Jail. "Common highlander." *SHS.3.80.*
McDONALD, WILLIAM, aged 40, a weaver, Drumnadeevan, Inverness-shire, McIntosh's Regiment. Imprisoned Inverness, June 1746 prison ship *James & Mary*, Medway. Transported 31.3.1747 to Barbados in *Frere*. *SHS.3.80, MR175, BMHS.30.80.*
McDONALD, WILLIAM, ?Captain, Clare's French Service. Imprisoned at sea, 28.11.1745 Berwick, February 1746 Hull, January 1747? Tower of London. Discharged. This may have been the "Capt McDonnel, French prisoner," who was in the Tower of London on 7 Jan 1747. *SHS.3.80.*
McDONALD, WILLIAM, farmer, aged 60. Imprisoned Carlisle. Transported 1747. *SHS.3.80.*
MacDONELL or MacDONALD, ALLAN, Reverend, released after June 1747. *SHS.1.224.*
MacDONELL or McDONELL, HUGH, Bishop, prisoner on parole until his death 1773. *SHS.1.224.*
MacDUGLE or MacDOUGALL, ALEXANDER, aged 26, from Inverness-shire. Lived with his father in... , *BMHS.30.80.*
MacDUGLE or MacDOUGALL, ALEXANDER, aged 26, from Ross-shire, tailor in Bullone. *BMHS.30.80.*
MacDUGLE or MacDOUGALL, JOHN, from Isle of ... Peddlar of Gainashel. *BMHS.30.80.*
McDOUALL or McDOUGALL, ALLAN (or ANGUS), "A blind Highland Pyper" from Argyll. Piper, Lord Nairn's (Duke of Atholl's Regiment). Imprisoned 17.1.1746 Falkirk,

20.1.1746 Leith, Edinburgh Jail. Released under General Pardon, 1747. "Says that he served as a piper to Lord Nairn's rebel regiment, and was taken at the battle of Falkirk." *SHS.2.233, SHS.3.80.*

McDOUALL, JOHN, from Argyll, Lochiel's Regiment. Imprisoned 1.11.1745 Kirkliston, Edinburgh Jail, 8.8.1746 Carlisle. "Common man." Deserted from the Prince's army. "This man is so sick that his confession could not be taken." There is no further reference to him. He probably died. *SHS.3.80.*

McDOUGALL, ALEXANDER or ALLAN, aged 26, gardener from Argyll. Duke of Perth's Regiment. Imprisoned 30.12.1745 Carlisle, York Castle. Transported Antigua 8.5.1747. Taken at the capture of Carlisle. *SHS.3.80.*

McDOUGAL or McDUGLE, ALEXANDER, aged 26, from Inverness, "lived with his father in Palencas." Lovat's Regiment. Imprisoned Inverness, Tilbury Fort. Transported 31.3.1747 from London to Barbados in *Frere*. *SHS.3.82, MR118.*

McDOUGAL, ALLAN, from Strathlachlan, Argyll, McLachlan's Regiment. Imprisoned 17.1.1746 surrendered at Fakkirk, 4.2.1746 Edinburgh, 8.8.1746, Carlisle, York Castle. Carrying baggage for McLachlan. Transported 31.3.1747 from Liverpool to Leeward Islands in *Veteran*, arriving Martinique June 1747. *SHS.3.82, MR181, PRO.SP36.102.*

McDOUGAL, ANGUS, Glengarry's Regiment. Imprisoned Aug 1746, HMS *Pamela*, Tilbury. He was apparently not transported, so he probably died. *SHS.3.82.*

McDOUGALL, HUGH, from Argyll, Duke of Perth's Regiment. Imprisoned 30.12.1745 Carlisle, York Castle, London (Southwark). Discharged. Taken at capture of Carlisle. He refused to swear the oath necessary for a commission, and was imprisoned by the Governor of Carlisle. He turned King's Evidence against the latter. *SHS.3.82.*

McDOUGAL or McDUGLE, JOHN, aged 26 from Ross, tailor in Bullone, Cromarty's Regiment. Imprisoned Inverness, June 1746 prison ship *Jane of Leith*, Tilbury Fort. Transported 20.3.1747. *SHS.3.82.*

McDOUGALL, JOHN, from Badenoch, Inverness-shire, Keppoch's Regiment. Imprisoned 17.3.1746 Edinburgh Castle, Edinburgh Tolbooth. Released under General Pardon, 1747. *SHS.3.82.*

McDOUGALL, JOHN, tennant to Robertson of Struan, origin Argyllshire, Lochiel's Regiment. Imprisoned Nov 1745 Monkland, 14.11.1745 Stirling Castle, Glasgow. Discharged 15.7.1747. *SHS.3.84.*

McDOUGALL, JOHN, aged 18 from Moidart, Clanranald's Regiment. Imprisoned Inverness, June 1746 prison ship *Wallsgrave*. He is not on the transportation lists, so he may have died. *SHS.3.84.*

McDOUGALL, JOHN, from Glenaladale, Moidart, Clanranald's Regiment. Imprisoned July 1746 Moidart, Dumbarton Castle, 4.2.1747 Glasgow. Released under General Pardon, 1747. "Served in Clanranald's rebel regiment until after the battle of Culloden, and was apprehended in Moidart by the Argyleshire levies." *SHS.3.84.*

McDOUGALL, or McDUGLE, JOHN, pedlar at Galnashel, Isle of Eigg, Clanranald's Regiment. Imprisoned Inverness, *Pamela*, Tilbury. Transported 31.3.1747 from London to Jamaica, in *St George or Carteret*, arriving Jamaica 1747. *SHS.3.84, MR143, PRO.CO137.58.*

McDOUGALL, NEILL, pilot from Scarinish, Isle of Tiree, McLean's Regiment. Imprisoned Aug 1746 Tiree, Dumbarton Castle, 4.2.1747 Glasgow. Discharged 15.7.1747. Says he "cannot tell in whose regiment, being only four days with rebels." "He was pilot to the French ships which came in to Lochnanaugh in Arisaig in May 1746 and was with McLean of Drimnin when levying men for the Pretender's service." *SHS.1.227, SHS.3.84.*

McEACHAIN or McGACHAN, CHARLES, Gentleman from Pennurin, South Uist. Imprisoned HMS *Furnace*, Tilbury, June 1746 in charge of a messenger. Discharged 11.6.1747. Charged with raising men. He turned King's Evidence against McDonald of Garifleuch. In or about June 1746 he was transferred to the custody of Mr Dick the messenger, where he stayed for a year. He was employed as a witness, and was discharged 11 June 1747. *SHS.3.86.*

McEACHAIN or McGACHAN, RONALD, from South Uist. Imprisoned HMS *Furnace*, Oct 1746 Tilbury. Discharged. "Son of O'Begg, an evidence." This entry suggests he was released. Albemarle says he was evidence against Clanranald and Benbecula. *SHS.3.86.*

McEACHINROY (McEACHAINRUADH), JOHN, from Kelso, Tiree, McLean's Regiment. Imprisoned Dumbarton Castle. Discharged July 1747. "Was in the rebellion and served

under McLean of Drimnin and continued with them until after
the battle of Culloden. *SHS.3.86.*
McELVENTIE (probably MacGillemhamtaigh), ANGUS,
Glengarry's Regiment. Imprisoned 30.12.1745 Carlisle.
Taken at capture of Carlisle. No reference to his disposal.
SHS.3.86.
McEVAN (McEWEN), JOHN, from Bellindrom, Glenmoriston,
Glengarry's Regiment. Imprisoned Inverness. "Of a
suspected character." Surrendered to Ludovic Grant. As
he is not in the list of Grants sent to London he was probably
released. *SHS.3.86.*
McEVAN (McEWEN), WILLIAM, from Invermoriston, Glenmoriston,
Glengarry's Regiment. Imprisoned 5.5.1746 Inverness.
"Returned after Gladsmuir and never rose any more in
arms." Surrendered to Ludovic Grant. *SHS.3.86.*
McEVAN, ROY ALEXANDER, from Wester Dundreggan,
Glenmoriston, Glengarry's Regiment. Imprisoned
Inverness. Surrendered to Ludovic Grant. *SHS.3.86.*
McFARLANE, JOHN, Roy Stuart's Regiment, drowned, Liverpool,
1 May 1747. *SHS.1.187.*
McIAN McFARQUHAR, FARQUHAR, from Wester Dundreggan,
Glenmoriston, Glengarry's Regiment. Imprisoned
Inverness. "Never in arms till March last." Surrendered to
Ludovic Grant. Not sent to London, and probably released.
SHS.3.88.
McFARQUHAR, KENNETH, aged 45, tenant farmer from Newton
of Redcastle, Ross-shire, Cromarty's Regiment. Imprisoned
Inverness, June 1746, prison ship *Wallsgrave*, Tilbury Fort.
Transported 31.3.1747 from London to Barbados in *Frere*.
"Was with the rebels and taken prisoner." *SHS.3.90, MR82,
BMHS.30.80.*
McGARRIE (MacGoraigh), ANGUS, from Inverness, Clanranald's
Regiment. Imprisoned 30.12.1745 Carlisle. Taken capture
at Carlisle. Nothing more is known of him. *SHS.3.90.*
McGILCHRIST, JOHN, Common highlander. Imprisoned on
suspicion Edinburgh Castle, 15.1.1746 Edinburgh.
Discharged July 1747. *SHS.3.90.*
McGILLIES, DANIEL (or Donald), elder, aged 60, labourer from
Arisaig, ?Glengarry's Regiment. Imprisoned Carlisle, York
Castle. Taken at capture of Carlisle. Transported Antigua
8.5.1747. *SHS.3.90, MR157.*
McGILLIES, DANIEL, younger, aged 14 from Arisaig, son of Daniel
McGillies, Glengarry's Regiment. Imprisoned Carlisle, York

Castle. Transported Antigua 8.5.1747 from Liverpool to Leeward Islands in *Veteran,* arriving Martinique June 1747. *SHS.3.90, MR158, PRO.SP36.102.*

McGILLIES, DONALD, aged 18, labourer from Inverness, Glengarry's Regiment. Imprisoned Carlisle, York Castle. Transported 5 May 1747 from Liverpool to Leeward Islands in *Veteran,* arriving Martinique June 1747. *SHS.3.90, MR158, PRO.SP36.102.*

McGILLIES, HECTOR, aged 16, herd from Inverness, Glengarry's Regiment. Imprisoned Carlisle, York Castle. Transported Antigua 8.5.1747 from Liverpool to Leeward Islands in *Veteran,* arriving Martinique June 1747. *SHS.3.90, MR158, PRO.SP26.102.*

McGILLIVRAY, ALEXANDER, of Dunmaglass, killed at Culloden *SHS.1.295.*

McGILLIVRAY, FARQUHAR, aged 50, farmer in Doghtsveire, Inverness-shire, McIntosh's Regiment. Imprisoned Inverness, Tilbury Fort. Was not transported. Probably died. *SHS.3.90.*

McGILPHADRICK, ANGUS, from Livicie, Glenmoriston, Glengarry's Regiment. Imprisoned Inverness. Surrendered to Ludovic Grant. As he was not sent to London, he was probably released. *SHS.3.90.*

McGINNIS (or McINNES), JOHN, from Skye. Imprisoned 11.7.1746 Ellagol, HMS *Furnace,* London (Tilbury), in a messenger's house. One of the Prince's boatmen, who fell into the hands of the barbarous Capt Ferguson, who "caused him to be stripped..... and whipped with the cat of nine tails till the blood gushed out if he did not discover where the Prince was." Nevertheless he turned King's Evidence against the Laird of Mackinnon and Mackinnon of Elgol. In April 1750 McKinnon of McKinnon told Bishop Forbes this man had been released and had returned home. *SHS.1.227, SHS.3.92.*

McGLUCKAN (perhaps MacLucas) RANALD, farmer in South Uist. Imprisoned Inverness, HMS prison ship *Pamela,* Tilbury Fort. Released April 1747. *SHS.3.92.*

McGRAW, DONALD, aged 24, farmer from Clochgolore, Ross-shire. Transported 20 Mar 1747 from London to Barbados in *Frere. SHS.3.182.*

McGREGOR, GREGOR, from Glenmoriston. Imprisoned Inverness. Escaped 1747. He was one of the gallant band of "Glenmoriston men" who took charge of the Prince in the later stages of his wanderings. He enlisted in Lord Loudon's regiment but deserted, and entertained the Prince at Coiraghoth. Some time after the troubles he was caught and imprisoned as a deserted in the Tolbooth, Inverness, but escaped. *SHS.3.92.*

McGRIGOR, GRIGOR, labourer from Argyllshire, Glengyle's Regiment. Imprisoned 15.11.1745 Ardno, 17.12.1745 Dumbarton. Liberated 21.8.1747. *SHS.3.92.*

McGRIGOR, JOHN, Glengyle's Regiment. Imprisoned 15.11.1745 Ardno, 17.11.1745 Dumbarton. Escaped 2.2.1746. *SHS.3.92.*

McGREGOR, JOHN, from Caithness, McDonald of Barisdale's Regiment. Imprisoned Aberdeen. Discharged. This man appears to have deserted as he was "putt ashoar here" (ie Aberdeen) "by the *Sheerness*, man of war. No witnesses against him." *SHS.3.94.*

McGREGOR, MARY, Keppoch's Regiment, released *SHS.1.216*

McGREGOR of Glencarnaig, ROBERT (alias Murray), Glengyle's Regiment. Imprisoned Inveraray, 6.3.1747 Edinburgh Castle. Released 11.10.1749. In hiding until September 1746 when he surrendered. Imprisoned in Edinburgh Castle for three years. Died 1758. He was "excepted" from the Act of Pardon. *SHS.3.96.*

McGREGOR, WILLIAM, aged 22, from Caithness, Cromarty's Regiment. Imprisoned Inverness, June 1746 prison ship *Thane of Fife*. The fact that he was not transported suggests that he died. *SHS.3.96.*

McHOMASH (MacThomais), PETER, from Craskie, Glenmoriston, Glengarry's Regiment. Imprisoned Inverness. "Made his escape from the south, again forced out and escaped, and a third time escaped from the north." Surrendered to Ludovic Grant. There is no evidence of what became of him. As he was apparently not sent to London he was probably released. *SHS.3.98.*

McHOULE (or Cameron), EVAN, from Lochaber. Shot. He had taken no part in the Rising. When the English troops visited Locharkaig he voluntarily surrendered his arms. He denied knowledge of the existence of any more arms, and was immediately shot in cold blood. *SHS.3.98.*

McHOULE, WILLIAM DOW, from Glenkengie. Shot. Was taken up on suspicion of having stolen a horst. A gun was found in his house, and he was shot on the spot. *SHS.3.98.*

McHOUSTON (MacHuisdein, Hughoson), DONALD, aged 40, from Caithness, Cromarty's Regiment. Imprisoned Inverness, June 1746 prison ship *Thane of Fife*, Tilbury. He was not transported, so perhaps he died. SHS.3.98.

McHUITCHEON (MacHuisdein), JOHN, aged 69, from Inverness, herded Lord Lovat's cattle, Lovat's Regiment. Imprisoned Inverness, HMS *James & Mary*, Medway. He is not shown in transportation lists, so he probably died. SHS.3.98.

McIAN VIC FARQUHAR, JOHN, from Wester Dundreggan, Glenmoriston, Glengarry's Regiment. Imprisoned Inverness. "Deserted after Falkirk and defied them afterwards to rise in arms." Surrendered to Ludovic Grant. He was probably released in due course. SHS.3.98.

McIGHAILL, JOHN, from Torosay, McGregor's of Glengyle's Regiment. Imprisoned in Dumbarton Castle. Discharged. "Taken immediately after the skirmish between General Campbell and Glengyle, but it was so dark none of the persons who apprehended him will be able to know him." SHS.3.98.

McINNES, ANDREW, aged 27, grazier at Tray, Morar, Inverness-shire, Clanranald's Regiment. Imprisoned Inverness, September 1746 prison ship *Pamela* Tilbury. Transported 30.3.1747. SHS.3.100, MR143.

McINTOSH, ANGUS, aged 26, from Inverness, McDonald of Glengarry's Regiment. Imprisoned 30.12.1745 Carlisle, York Castle. Transported Antigua 8.5.1747 from Liverpool to Leeward Islands in *Veteran*, arriving Martinique June 1747. Taken at capture of Carlisle. SHS.3.100, PRO.SP36.102.

McINTOSH, Lady, The Dowager, ANNE, aged 21. Imprisoned April 1746 Inverness. Released May 1746. Daughter of colin Mackenzie of Redcastle. Bailie John Stuart, Inverness, describing the treatment of the inhabitants after Cumberland's arrival there, says "the women of Inverness did not escape his royal highness his notice. Several of them were made prisoners and confined to the common guard amongst whom was the Dowager Lady Mackintosh, who was confined for the space of 14 days, and contracted so violent a cold during that time that she had almost died of it. SHS.3.100.

McINTOSH, Lady ANNE, from Moy, Inverness. Imprisoned Moy House, Inverness. Released 1746. Anne, daughter of James Farquharson, 9th of Invercauld, was born 1723. She married Angus of Aeneas Mackintosh, 22nd of Mackintosh, who, though a Jacobite Peer as 3rd Lord McIntosh, and theoretically a Jacobite, refused to come out and raised a company for the Government. His wife, on the other hand, raised many of the clan, the McBeans and the McGillivrays, for the Prince, and put Alexander McGillivray or Dunmaglass to command them. Through her vigilance the Prince escaped capture at her house at Moy on 16 Feb 1746. She was arrested after Culloden, and taken to Inverness, but was released six weeks later through her husband's influence. She died in 1787. *SHS.3.102.*

McINTOSH, ANN, aged 20, from Inverness, "knits and spins." Taken at capture of Carlisle. Imprisoned 30.12.1745 Carlisle, Lancaster Castle. Transported to Antigua 8.5.1747 *SHS.1.217, SHS.3.102.*

McINTOSH, DANIEL, from Argyll, Glengarry's Regiment. Imprisoned 30.12.1745, taken at the capture of Carlisle. No further reference to him. *SHS.2.102.*

McINTOSH, DUNCAN, carpenter, aged 60, from near Inverness, Duke of Perth's Regiment. Imprisoned 30.12.1745 Carlisle, Lancaster Castle. Taken at the capture of Carlisle. Transported from Liverpool to Virginia on *Johnston*, arriving Port Oxford, Maryland, 5 Aug 1747. Returned to Scotland 1748. *SHS.3.102, MR74, PRO.T1.328.*

McINTOSH, JOHN, aged 51, fiddler from Inverness, Duke of Perth's Regiment. Imprisoned Carlisle, Lancaster Castle. Transported Antigua 5.8.1747 from Liverpool to Leeward Islands in *Veteran*, arriving Martinique June 1747. *SHS.3.102, PRO.SP36.102, MR74.*

McINTOSH, JOHN, McIntosh's Regiment, died at Tilbury, 12 June 1747. *SHS.1.187, SHS.3.102.*

MacINTOSH, LACHLAN, aged 22, Tailor Merchant of Inverness, Lieutenant Colonel, Lovat's Regiment. Captured at Culloden, imprisoned Inverness, June 1746 prison ship *Margaret & Mary*, hospital ship *Liberty & Property*, Medway. Transported 31.3.1747 from London to Barbados in *Frere*. This was the Inverness merchant who "was a Lt Col and enlisted many men." He was included in the first Bill of Attainder. Albemarle, in a letter, 28 Oct 1746, to the Duke of Newcastle, said he heard this man was living in the house of Alexander McIntosh, a draper in London, and recommended his arrest. *SHS.1.295, SHS.3.102, BMHS.30.80.*

McINTOSH, PETER, aged 34, labourer from Inverness, Duke of Perth's Regiment. Imprisoned Carlisle, York Castle. Transportd Antigua 8.5.1747 from Liverpool to Leeward Islands in *Veteran*, arriving Martinique June 1747. *SHS.3.102, MR74, PRO.SP36.102.*

McINTOSH, WILLIAM, aged 30, a pedlar from Nairn, "origin Inverness," McIntosh's Regiment. Imprisoned Inverness, June 1746 prison ship *Jane of Alloway*, Tilbury Fort. "Was a baggage man, a poor object." He was not transported, and may have died at Tilbury. *SHS.3.104.*

McINTYRE, ANN, aged 30, from Argyllshire. Imprisoned Carlisle 30.12.1745. Transported to Antigua 8.5.1747. Captured at fall of Carlisle. *SHS.1.217, SHS.3.104.*

McINTYRE, ARCHIBALD, aged 50, lead miner from Argyllshire. Imprisoned York Castle, Lincoln Castle. Transported 22.4.1747 from Liverpool to Virginia in *Johnson*, arriving Port Oxford, Maryland, 5 August 1747. *SHS.3.104, PRO.T1.328.*

McINTYRE, DONALD, aged 56, "quack doctor" from Argyllshire. Imprisoned Carlisle, Lancaster Castle. Transported 22 Apr 1747 from Liverpool to Virginia in *Johnson*, arriving Port Oxford, Maryland, 5 Aug 1747. He was taken prisoner at Carlisle. *SHS.1.220, SHS.3.104, PRO.T1.328.*

McINTYRE, DUNCAN, aged 42, brewer from Lochielhead, Stewart of Ardshiel's Regiment. Imprisoned Inverness, June 1746 hospital ship *Liberty & Property*, Tilbury. Transported 20 Mar 1747. *SHS.3.104, MR14, BMHS.30.80.*

McINTYRE, JOHN, from Argyll. Imprisoned 16.4.1746 Culloden, Inverness. "Bawman to the Pretender." His fate is unknown; not shown in any of the transports. He probably died. *SHS.3.104.*

McINTYRE, JOHN, from Craskie, Glenmoriston, Glengarry's Regiment. Imprisoned 5.5.1746 Inverness, Tilbury. "Suspected a thief." Surrendered to Ludovic Grant. He probably died, as he was not transported. *SHS.3.106*

McINTYRE, MARY, Imprisoned 30.12.1745 Carlisle. Transported Antigua 8.5.1747. Taken at the fall of Carlisle. *SHS.1.217, SHS.3.106.*

McINTYRE, PATRICK, from Argyllshire. Imprisoned 13.6.1746 Perth. Discharged on bail 13.7.1746. Rebel service. *SHS.3.106.*

McINVINE (MacFhionghuin, Mackinnon), DONALD, from Mull, Cromarty's Regiment. Imprisoned Dumbarton Castle. Discharged. "Denies that he was in the rebellion. Can give no distinct account of himself. Guilty of habitual stealing." *SHS.3.106.*

McIVOR, EVANDER, aged 20, from Ross, Cromarty's Regiment. Imprisoned Inverness, Tilbury Fort. Lived with his father in Ishinishish. No reference to his being transported. May have died. *SHS.3.106.*

McIVOR, DONALD, aged 21 from Ross, Cromarty's Regiment. Imprisoned Inverness, June 1746 prison ship *Alexander & James*, Tilbury. *SHS.3.106.*

McIVOR, DANIEL or DONALD, aged 24 from Ross, Cromarty's Regiment. Imprisoned Inverness, June 1746 prison ship *Alexander & James* Tilbury Fort. Discharged. Farmer in Dunnomuch. Employed as a witness. *SHS.3.106.*

McIVOR, or McEver, KENNETH, aged 22, from Sutherland, Cromarty's Regiment. Imprisoned Inverness, June 1746 prison ship *Alexander & James*. *SHS.3.106.*

McKAY, ANDREW, McIntosh's Regiment. Imprisoned Canongate, 8.8.1746 Carlisle. Died in Carlisle Prison 15.6.1747. *SHS.1.187, SHS.3.106.*

McKAY, or McLeod, ANNE, from Skye. Imprisoned Inverness, released April 1747. She was in Inverness in the house in which Robert Nairn and McDonald of Belfinlay were put after they were brought in wounded from Culloden. She assisted in a plot laid by certain ladies to help Nairn escape. She was captured and imprisoned in the Tolbooth, and sentenced to be whipped through the town; but this was prevented through interest brought to bear on the military authorities. She was, however, for some time not allowed to sit or lie down, in order to get her to confess the names of her associates. This she refused to do. After some weeks she was released. *SHS.3.106.*

McKAY, DONALD, from Achmonie, Glen Urquhart, Inverness-shire, Glengarry's Regiment. Imprisoned 5.5.1746 Inverness, June 1746 prison ship *Jane of Alloway*, transported to Barbados, settled Jamaica. Youngest brother of Alexander McKay of Achmonie. Surrendered 5 May to Ludovic Grant of Grant, and was imprisoned and sent to London. He was one of the few who succeeded in returning to Scotland. He escaped as a stowaway to Jamaica, assumed the name of McDonald, and became a planter. Long after he returned home and married. *SHS.108, MR150.*

McKAY, DUNCAN, labourer from Castle Doune, Perthshire, "origin Inverness", Ogilvie's Regiment. Imprisoned 30.12.1745 Carlisle, Chester Castle, York Castle. Transported 1747. Taken at capture of Carlisle. *SHS.3.108, MR105.*
MacKAY, JAMES, Glengarry's Regiment. Imprisoned 7.9.1745 St Ninians, Carlisle, Chester Castle. Sentenced to be transported, but was drowned at Liverpool when going on board a ship for transportation 2 May 1747 (or March 1747). *SHS.1.187, SHS.3.108.*
McKAY, JOHN, aged 34, from Inverness, Glengarry's Regiment. Imprisoned Inverness, June 1746 prison ship *Alexander & James*, Tilbury. No reference to his being transported; may have died in Tilbury. *SHS.3.108.*
McKAY, ROBERT, aged 25, from Sutherland, McGregor of Glengyle's Regiment. Imprisoned Inverness, Tilbury Fort. Discharged. Servant to Jno. Sutherland. This was probably the man who gave evidence against several prisoners at the trials at Southward. *SHS.3.110.*
McKAY, ROBERT, aged 20, from Dornoch, Lord Lewis Gordon's Regiment. Imprisoned Inverness, June 1746, prison ship *Jane of Leith*, Tilbury. Transported 1747. *SHS.3.110, MR128.*
McKAY, ROBERT, aged 22, from Sutherland, Lord Lewis Gordon's Regiment. Imprisoned Inverness, June 1746 prison ship *Wallsgrave*, Tilbury Fort. Transported 1747. Cooper in Fochabers. *SHS.3.110, MR128.*
McKAY, TASKEL, aged 20 (60?), from Inverness, Cromarty's Regiment. Imprisoned Inverness, June 1746 prison ship *Liberty*, Medway. Transported 31.3.1747. "Formerly soldier in Lord Loudon's (McLeod's Company). *SHS.3.110, MR83, BMHS.30.80.*
McKENZIE, ALEXANDER, of Corry, aged 40, from Thurso, Caithness, Lieutenant, Cromarty's Regiment. Imprisoned Dunrobin, Inverness, Tilbury Fort, 23.10.1746 Southward. Transported 31.3.1747 from London to Barbados in *Frere*. "Lord Cromarty's Factor lived at Corry." Captured at Dunrobin. He was tried 22 Jan 1747 and sentenced to death, but reprieved on 12 February. *SHS.3.110, MR79, BMHS.30.80.*
McKENZIE, ALEXANDER, aged 23, from Ross, Cromarty's Regiment. Imprisoned Inverness, June 1746, prison ship *Jane of Leith*, Tilbury Fort. Transported 31.3.1747 from

London to Barbados, in *Frere*. Servant to Jennet McKenzie, Bracklock. *SHS.3.112, MR83, BMHS.30.80*.

McKENZIE, ALEXANDER, aged 50, farmer in Aghandreine, Ross-shire, Cromarty's Regiment. Imprisoned Inverness, June 1746 prison ship *Thane of Fife*, Tilbury Fort. Transported 31.3.1747 from London to Barbados in *Frere*. *SHS.3.112, MR83, BMHS.30.81*.

McKENZIE, ALEXANDER, aged 22, servant to McKenzie in Ballachriche, Ross-shire, Cromarty's Regiment. Imprisoned Inverness, Tilbury Fort. Transported 31.3.1747 from London to Barbados in *Frere*. *SHS.3.112, MR83*.

McKENZIE, ALEXANDER, aged 28, from Coull, Coutrie, Ross-shire, Cromarty's Regiment. Imprisoned July 1746 Inverness, July 1746 prison ship *Pamela*, Tilbury. Transported 31.3.1747 from London to Jamaica in *St George or Carteret*, arriving Jamaica 1747. Grieve to Mackenzie of Balmudathy. "Was employed in forcing out men into the Rebellion...... by his late Master's orders. Now prisoner in Inverness." He submitted an appeal stating that he had had nothing to do with the rebellion, and that his arrest was due to the ill-will of one Lewis Rae. He also said that he had been induced to sign the petition for mercy and transportation under misapprehension. His appeal must have been rejected as he was transported. *SHS.3.112, MR83, BMHS.30.81*.

McKENZIE, ALEXANDER, aged 18 (13?), tailor from Argyllshire, Cromarty's Regiment. Imprisoned Falkirk, Inverness, June 1746 prison ship *Alexander & James*, hospital ship *Liberty & Property*, Tilbury. Transported 31.3.1747 from London to Barbados in *Frere*. "Was in the King's army" and therefore a deserter. Taken prisoner at Falkirk. *SHS.3.112, MR83, BMHS.30.81*.

McKENZIE, ALEXANDER, aged 24, from Ross, Cromarty's Regiment. Imprisoned Inverness, June 1746 prison ship *Alexander & James*, prison ship *Liberty*, Tilbury. Transported 31.3.1747. *SHS.2.112, BMHS.30.81*.

McKENZIE, ALEXANDER, aged 28, from Ross, Cromarty's Regiment. Imprisoned Inverness, June 1746 prison ship *Jane of Leith*, HMS *Liberty & Property*, Medway. Transported 31.3.1747 from London to Jamaica in *St George or Carteret*, arriving Jamaica 1747. Sold snuff in Logie. *SHS.3.112, MR83, PRO.CO137.58, BMHS.30.81*.

McKENZIE, ALEXANDER, aged 30, from Cromarty, Cromarty's Regiment. Imprisoned Inverness, June 1746 prison ship *Jane of Leith*. Transported 31.3.1747 from London to Jamaica in *St George or Carteret*, arriving Jamaica 1747. *SHS.3.114, MR83, PRO.CO.137.58, BMHS.30.81.*

MacKENZIE, ALEXANDER, aged 40, from Cromarty. *BMHS.30.81.*

McKENZIE, ALEXANDER, aged 32, from Cromarty, Cromarty's Regiment. Imprisoned Inverness, June 1746 prison ship *Jane of Leith*. Transported 31.3.1747 from London to Jamaica in *St George or Carteret*, arriving Jamaica 1747. *SHS.3.114, MR83, PRO.CO.137.58.*

McKENZIE, ALEXANDER or SANDERS, aged 28, labourer in Lord Cromarty's, Ross-shire, Cromarty's Regiment. Imprisoned Inverness, Tilbury Fort. As he was not transported with the others, he probably died at Tilbury. *SHS.3.114.*

McKENZIE, ALEXANDER, aged 24, Clanranald's Regiment. Imprisoned Inverness, HMS *Pamela*, Tilbury. Transported 31.3.1747 from Tilbury. *SHS.3.114.*

McKENZIE, ALEXANDER, aged 25, husbandry in Drumhardinich, Inverness-shire, Lovat's Regiment. Imprisoned Inverness, June 1746 prison ship *Margaret & Mary*, prison ship *James & Mary*, Medway. Transported 1747. *SHS.3.114, MR119.*

McKENZIE, ANDREW, aged 36, from Cromarty, Cromarty's Regiment. Imprisoned Inverness, June 1746 prison ship *Jane of Leith*. Disposal unknown, but was not transported. Probably died at Tilbury. *SHS.3.114.*

McKENZIE, ANGUS, Glengarry's Regiment. Imprisoned Inverness May 1746 prison ship *Jane of Leith*. Died on *Jane of Leith*, 2 June 1746 *SHS.1.188, SHS.3.114.*

McKENZIE, ANNE, aged 60, knitter from Glengarry, Inverness-shire. Imprisoned 30.12.1745 Carlisle, Lancaster Castle. Transported 22.4.1747 from Liverpool to Virginia in *Johnson*, arriving Port Oxford, Maryland, 5 Aug 1747. Taken at capture of Carlisle. *SHS.1.217, SHS.3.114, PRO.T1.328.*

McKENZIE, ARCHIBALD, aged 18, herd, Glengarry's Regiment. Imprisoned Stirling Castle. Transported 1747. *SHS.3.114, MR158.*

McKENZIE, COLIN of Ballone, Captain, aged 20, from Lochbroom, Cromarty's Regiment. Imprisoned Dunrobin, Inverness June 1746, prison ship *Thane of Fife*, Tilbury, Southward. Acquitted 8.11.1746. He was opposed to the Rising and was eventualy forced to join. Captured at Dunrobin. He

was tried in London 8.11.1746. The Rev James Robertson, Lochbroom, showed that he was well disposed to the Government and interceded with Cumberland for him. Other witnesses proved he had taken arms against Barisdale when the latter tried to force him out. He was acquitted. SHS.3.116.
McKENZIE, DANIEL, aged 33 (40), servant to Donald Mair, Curmigh, Inverness-shire, Barisdale's Regiment. Imprisoned Inverness, June 1746 prison ship Wallsgrave, Tilbury Fort. Transported 1747 from Tilbury. SHS.3.116.MR158.
McKENZIE, DANIEL, aged 19, lived with his father in Aghterscaild, Ross-shire, Cromarty's Regiment. Imprisoned Inverness, Tilbury Fort. Not shown as transported, probably died at Tilbury. SHS.3.116.
McKENZIE, (alias Gow) DANIEL, aged 19, blacksmith's apprentice from Ross-shire, Cromarty's Regiment. Imprisoned Inverness, Tilbury Fort. Not show as transported, probably died at Tilbury Fort. SHS.3.116.
McKENZIE, DAVID, aged 30, from Ross-shire, Cromarty's Regiment. Imprisoned Inverness, June 1746 prison ship *Jane of Leith*, Tilbury. Not shown as as transported, probably died at Tilbury. SHS.3.116.
McKENZIE, DONALD, Captain?, Cromarty's Regiment. Imprisoned 17.3.1747 Edinburgh Castle, London. Transported 1747. This is probably Donald McKenzie, tenant of Invahanny, Inverness, who "was a Captain under Cromarty." He appears to have been sent to London, and was there in 1748. He was ultimately transported. SHS.3.116, MR79.
McKENZIE, DONALD, from Lochaber. Imprisoned July 1746 Canongate. "Change keeper at Tynadreen, Lochaber." No further report. SHS.3.116.
McKENZIE, DONALD, aged 38, labourer. Imprisoned Carlisle. Transported 21.7.1748. "Common man." Taken at capture of Carlisle. He was tried on 19 Sept 1746, pleaded guilty, and was sentenced to death. SHS.3.116.
McKENZIE, DONALD, from Ballachulish, Argyll, Lochiel's Regiment. Imprisoned Feb 1746 Clifton Dumbarton, 4.2.1747 Glasgow. Discharged 15.7.1747. "At the battles of Preston and Falkirk." SHS.3.116.
McKENZIE, DONALD, aged 40, farmer from Badralloch, Lochbroom, Ross-shire, Cromarty's Regiment. Imprisoned

Inverness, Tilbury Fort. Transported 31.3.47 from London to
Jamaica in *St George or Carteret*, arriving Jamaica 1747.
SHS.3.118, MR83, PRO.CO137.58, BMHS.30.81.

McKENZIE, DONALD, aged 25, from Ross-shire, Cromarty's
Regiment. Imprisoned Inverness, June 1746 prison ship
Thane of Fife, Tilbury Fort. Transported 31.3.1747 from
London to Jamaica in *St George or Carteret*, arriving
Jamaica 1747. Lived with his father near Castle Leod.
SHS.3.118, MR83, PRO.CO.137.58, BMHS.30.81.

McKENZIE, DONALD, aged 40, farmer in Ballevloide, Ross-shire,
Cromarty's Regiment. Imprisoned Inverness, Tilbury Fort.
Transported 31.3.1747 from London to Barbados in *Frere*.
SHS.3.118, MR83, BMHS.30.81.

McKENZIE, DONALD, aged 57, Cromarty's Regiment.
Imprisoned Inverness, Tilbury Fort. Transported 31.3.1747
from Tilbury. *SHS.3.118, BMHS.30.81.*

McKENZIE, DONALD, aged 20, from Ross-shire, Cromarty's
Regiment. Imprisoned Inverness, June 1746 prison ship
Jane of Leith, Tilbury Fort. Transported 31.3.1747 from
London to Barbados in *Frere*. *SHS.3.118, MR83,
BMHS.30.81.*

McKENZIE, DONALD, aged 36, Cromarty's Regiment.
Imprisoned Inverness, Tilbury Fort. Transported 31.3.1747
from London to Barbados in *Frere*. *SHS.3.118, MR83.*

McKENZIE, DONALD, aged 20, husbandman at Ballene, Ross-shire, Cromarty's Regiment. Imprisoned Inverness, June
1746 prison ship *Alexander & James,* hospital ship *Liberty &
Property*, Medway. Transported 20.3.1747. *SHS.3.118,
MR83, BMHS.30.81.*

McKENZIE, DONALD, aged 35, husbandman from Letanochglass,
Ross-shire, Cromarty's Regiment. Imprisoned Inverness,
June 1746 prison ship *Jane of Alloway*, Tilbury, prison ship
Liberty. Transported 19.3.1747 from Tilbury. *SHS.3.118,
MR83, BMHS.30.81.*

McKENZIE, DONALD, aged 30, Barisdale's Regiment.
Imprisoned Inverness, Tilbury Fort. Transported 20.3.1747.
SHS.3.118, MR158.

McKENZIE, DONALD, aged 25, from Inverness, Lovat's Regiment.
Imprisoned Inverness, June 1746 prison ship *Alexander &
James*. Transported 20.3.1747. *SHS.3.118, MR119.*

McKENZIE, DUNCAN, "Rebel Service" Deserter from the Scots
Fusiliers, taken at Culloden. Imprisoned 17.4.1746
Culloden, hanged 28.4.1746. *SHS.3.118.*

McKENZIE, DUNCAN, tailor at Ferry House near Lochiels, origin Argyllshire, Lochiel's Regiment. Imprisoned Sept 1746 HMS prison ship *Pamela* Tilbury. Transported 1747. *SHS.3.118, MR35.*

McKENZIE, DUNCAN, from Ballachulish, Lochiel's Regiment. Imprisoned Feb 1746Clifton,Dumbarton Castle, 4.2.1747 Glasgow. Discharged 15.7.1747. "At Preston and Falkirk." *SHS.3.120.*

McKENZIE, DUNCAN, aged 27, husbandman in the lands of the Laird of Ballone, Ross-shire, Cromarty's Regiment. Imprisoned Inverness, June 1746 prison ships *Thane of Fife, Liberty,* Tilbury. Transported 31.3.1747 from London to Jamaica in *St George or Carteret,* arriving Jamaica 1747. *SHS.2.120, MR83, PRO.T1.328, BMHS.30.81.*

McKENZIE, DUNCAN, aged 40, farmer from Braemore, Ross-shire, Cromarty's Regiment. Imprisoned Inverness, June 1746 prison ships *Thane of Fife, James & Mary,* Tilbury. Transported 20.3.1747 from Tilbury. *SHS.3.120, MR83.*

McKENZIE, DUNCAN, aged 54, from Ross-shire, Cromarty's Regiment. Imprisoned Inverness, June 1746 prison ship *Thane of Fife,* Tilbury. Not transported, probably died. *SHS.3.120.*

McKENZIE, DUNCAN, aged 18, from Ross-shire, Cromarty's Regiment. Imprisoned Inverness, June 1746 prison ship *Jane of Leith,* Tilbury. Transported 1747. *SHS.3.120.*

McKENZIE, DUNCAN, aged 20, from Ross-shire, Cromarty's Regiment. Imprisoned Inverness, June 1746 prison ship *Jane of Leith,* Tilbury. Transported 1747. *SHS.3.120, MR83.*

McKENZIE, DUNCAN, aged 26, from Cromarty, Ross-shire, Cromarty's Regiment. Imprisoned Inverness, June 1746 prison ship *Jane of Leith.* Transported 1747. *SHS.3.120, MR83.*

McKENZIE, FINLAY, aged 54, from Ross-shire, Cromarty's Regiment. Imprisoned Inverness, June 1746 prison ship *Margaret & Mary.* No reference to transportation, probably died. *SHS.3.120.*

McKENZIE, FLORA, imprisoned 30.12.1745 Carlisle, Lancaster Castle. Wife of Donald McKenzie. Taken at capture of Carlisle. Fate unknown. *SHS.1.217, SHS.3.120.*

McKENZIE, GEORGE, aged 32 (33?), from Ross-shire, Cromarty's Regiment. Imprisoned Inverness, June 1746 prison ship *Alexander & James,* Tilbury Fort. Transported 31.3.1747 from London to Barbados in *Frere*. Served under Sir Rory McKenzie. *SHS.3.122, MR84, BMHS.30.81.*

McKENZIE, GEORGE, aged 21, servant to Thomas Urquhart, Glasslau, Ross-shire, Cromarty's Regiment. Imprisoned Inverness, June 1746 prison ship *Jane of Leith*, Tilbury Fort. Transported 20.3.1747 from Tilbury. *SHS.3.122, MR84.*

McKENZIE, GEORGE, aged 32, farmer in Coigach, Ross-shire, Cromarty's Regiment. Imprisoned Inverness, June 1746 prison ship *Jane of Leith, Liberty & Property*, Medway. Transported 1747. *SHS.3.122, MR84.*

McKENZIE, HECTOR, aged 45, from Lochbroom, Ross-shire, Ensign, Cromarty's Regiment. Imprisoned Inverness, June 1746 prison ship *Thane of Fife*, London (Southwark). Pardoned conditionally on banishment to America, 13.10.1748. Forester to Lord Cromarty. He claimed duress and made frequent efforts to escape. He was tried in London and sentenced to death. By the intercession of Rev James Robertson, Lochbroom, with the Duke of Cumberland, he was pardoned and released on condition of leaving the country permanently and "transporting himself to America." Transported Oct 1748. *SHS.3.122.*

McKENZIE, HUGH, from Mull. Imprisoned Dumbarton Castle, released under General Pardon 1747. "Denies that he was in the rebellion. Can give no distinct account of himslef. Guilty of habitual stealing." *SHS.3.122.*

McKENZIE, JAMES, aged 22, tailor in Oolder Hooste, origin Inverness, McIntosh's Regiment. Imprisoned Inverness, June 1746 prison ship *Jane of Alloway*, Tilbury Fort. Transported 31.3.1747 from London to Barbados in *Frere*. *SHS.3.122, MR84, BMHS.30.81.*

McKENZIE, JAMES, aged 20, from Inverness, Cromarty's Regiment. Imprisoned Inverness, June 1746 prison ship *Alexander & James*. Transported 20.3.1747. *SHS.3.122, MR84.*

McKENZIE, JAMES, aged 20, joiner from Suddie, Ross-shire, Cromarty's Regiment. Imprisoned Inverness, June 1746 prison ships *Jane of Alloway, Liberty & Property*, Medway. Transported 31.3.1747. *SHS.3.122, BMHS.30.81.*

McKENZIE, JEAN or Jane, aged 19, "knits sews and washes" from Inverness, taken at capture of Carlisle. Imprisoned 30.12.1745 Carlisle, York Castle. Transported Antigua 8.5.1747 from Liverpool to Leeward Islands in *Veteran*, arriving Martinique June 1747. *SHS.1.217, SHS.3.124, MR84.*

McKENZIE, JOHN, aged 22, from Ardloch, Assynt, "Gentleman – obliged to go" Captain, Cromarty's Regiment. Imprisoned Carlisle, Lancaster Castle. Transported Antigua 8.5.1747, from Liverpool to Leeward islands, in *Veteran,* arriving Martinique June 1747. *SHS.124, MR79, PRO.SP36.102.*

McKENZIE, JOHN, aged 40, farmer in Dornoch, Ross-shire, Cromarty's Regiment. Imprisoned Inverness, June 1746 prison ship *Thane of Fife,* Tilbury Fort. Transported 31.3.1747 from London to Barbados in *Frere SHS.3.124, MR84, BMHS.30.81.*

McKENZIE, JOHN, aged 50, husbandman from Dingwall, Rosshire, Cromarty's Regiment. Imprisoned Inverness, June 1746 prison ship *Thane of Fife,* Tilbury Fort. Transported 31.3.1747 from London to Barbados in *Frere. SHS.3.124, BMHS.30.81.*

McKENZIE, JOHN, aged 20, servant to Mr Dingwall in Strathpeffer, Ross-shire, Cromarty's Regiment. Imprisoned Inverness, June 1746 prison ship *Thane of Fife,* Tilbury Fort. Transported 31.3.1747 from London to Barbados in *Frere. SHS.3.124, MR84, BMHS.30.81.*

McKENZIE, JOHN, aged 38, servant to John Stuart, origin Ross-shire, Cromarty's Regiment. Imprisoned Inverness, June 1746 prison ship *Margaret & Mary,* Tilbury Fort. Transported 31.3.1747 from London to Barbados in *Frere. SHS.3.124, MR84, BMHS.30.81.*

McKENZIE, JOHN, aged 28, lived with his father at Aughtermead, Ross-shire, Cromarty's Regiment. Imprisoned Inverness, June 1746 prison ship *Jane of Leith,* Tilbury Fort. Transported 31.3.1747 from London to Jamaica in *St George or Carteret,* arriving Jamaica 1747. *SHS.3.124, MR84, PRO.CO137.58, BMHS.30.81.*

McKENZIE, JOHN, aged 56, farmer in Dormie, Ross-shire, Cromarty's Regiment. Imprisoned Inverness, June 1746 prison ship *Jane of Leith,* Tilbury Fort. Transported 31.3.1747 from London to Jamaica in *St George or Carteret,* arriving Jamaica 1747. *SHS.3.124, MR84, PRO.CO137.58, BMHS.30.81.*

McKENZIE, JOHN, aged 20, weaver from Aghtonshiel, (Achnashiel) Ross-shire, Cromarty's Regiment. Imprisoned Inverness, June 1746 prison ship *Alexander & James,*

Tilbury Fort. Transported 31.3.1747 from London to
Barbados in *Frere. SHS.3.124, MR84, BMHS.30.81.*

McKENZIE, JOHN, aged 36, farmer under Lord Cromarty, Ashlet,
Ross-shire, Cromarty's Regiment. Imprisoned Inverness,
June 1746 prison ships *Thane of Fife, Liberty, Medway.*
Transported 20.3.1747. *SHS.3.124, MR84.*

McKENZIE, JOHN, aged 45, farmer in lands of McKenzie of
Auchterdonald, Ross-shire, Cromarty's Regiment.
Imprisoned Inverness, June 1746 prison ships *Wallsgrave,
James & Mary,* Medway. Transported 20.3.1747.
SHS.3.126.

McKENZIE, JOHN, aged 40, farmer in Logie, Ross-shire,
Cromarty's Regiment. Imprisoned Inverness, June 1746
prison ships *Jane of Leith, James & Mary,* Medway.
Transported 20.3.1747. *SHS.3.126, MR84.*

McKENZIE, JOHN, aged 38, farmer in Micklestrath, Ross-shire,
Cromarty's Regiment. Imprisoned Inverness, June 1746
prison ships *Alexander & James, James & Mary,* Medway.
Disposal unknown, probably died. *SHS.3.126.*

McKENZIE, JOHN, aged 18, servant to Colin McKenzie in Logie,
Ross-shire, a rebel, Cromarty's Regiment. Imprisoned
Inverness, June 1746 prison ships *Jane of Leith, Liberty,*
Medway. Transported 20.3.1747. *SHS.3.126, MR.84.*

McKENZIE, JOHN, aged 27, from Cromarty, Cromarty's Regiment.
Imprisoned Inverness, June 1746 prison ship *Jane of Leith.*
Transported 1747. *SHS.3.126, MR84.*

McKENZIE, JOHN, aged 32, from Cromarty, Cromarty's Regiment.
Imprisoned Inverness, June 1746 prison ship *Jane of Leith.*
No reference to being transported, probably died.
SHS.3.126.

McKENZIE, JOHN, from Ballachulish, Argyll, Glengarry's
Regiment. Imprisoned Carlisle. "Carried arms. Prisoner."
Pardoned on condition of enlistment 22.7.1748. Pleaded
guilty at his trial, 19 Sept 1746, and was sentenced to death,
but reprieved. *SHS.3.126.*

McKENZIE, KENNETH, aged 22, "servant to the Minister, Contin,"
Ross-shire, Barisdale's Regiment. Imprisoned June 1746
prison ships *Jane of Leith, Liberty,* Medway. Transported
31.3.1747 from London to Barbados in *Frere. SHS.3.128,
MR158, BMHS.30.81.*

McKENZIE, KENNETH, aged 38, servant to Alexander Mansel,
Ross-shire, Cromarty's Regiment. Imprisoned Inverness,
June 1746 prison ship *Jane of Leith,* Tilbury Fort.

Transported 31.3.1747 from London to Jamaica in *St George or Carteret*, arriving Jamaica 1747. *SHS.3.128, MR85, PRO.CO137.58, BMHS.30.81.*

McKENZIE, KENNETH, aged 26, lived with his father in Lochbroom, Ross-shire, Cromarty's Regiment. Imprisoned Inverness, June 1746 prison ship *Wallsgrave*, Tilbury Fort. Transported 31.3.1747 from London to Barbados in *Frere*. *SHS.3.128, MR84, BMHS.30.82.*

McKENZIE, KENNETH, aged 32, managed a farm for his mother in Bullon, Ross-shire, Cromarty's Regiment. Imprisoned Inverness, June 1746 prison ship *Alexander & James*, Tilbury Fort. Transported 31.3.1747 from London to Barbados in *Frere*. *SHS.3.128, MR84, BMHS.30.82.*

McKENZIE, KENNETH, aged 55, farmer in Invervaigh, Lochbroom, Ross-shire, Cromarty's Regiment. Imprisoned Inverness, June 1746 prison ship *Alexander & James*, Tilbury Fort. Transported 19.3.1747 from Tilbury to Jamaica in *St George or Carteret*, arriving Jamaica 1747. *SHS.3.128, MR84, PRO.CO137.58.*

McKENZIE, KENNETH, aged 30, husbandman on lands of Laird of Ballon, Ross-shire, Cromarty's Regiment. Imprisoned Inverness, June 1746 prison ships *Thane of Fife, Liberty, Medway*. Transported 31.3.1747 from London to Jamaica in *St George or Carteret*, arriving Jamaica 1747. *SHS.3.128, PRO.CO137.58, BMHS.30.82.*

McKENZIE, KENNETH, aged 19, husbandman from Little Strath, Ross-shire, Cromarty's Regiment. Imprisoned Inverness, June 1746 prison ships *Thane of Fife, James & Mary*. Transported 31.3.1747 from London to Barbados in *Frere*. *SHS.3.128, MR84, BMHS.30.82.*

McKENZIE, KENNETH, aged 30, farmer in Aschellach, Ross-shire, Cromarty's Regiment. Imprisoned Inverness, June 1746 prison ships *Jane of Leith, James & Mary*, Tilbury. Transported 20.3.1747. *SHS.3.128, MR.84, BMHS.30.82.*

McKENZIE, KENNETH, aged 19, husbandman in Lochmallin, Ross-shire, Cromarty's Regiment. Imprisoned Inverness, June 1746 prison ships *Thane of Fife, Liberty, Medway*. Transported 19.3.1747. *SHS.3.130, MR85.*

McKENZIE, KENNETH, aged 21, from Ross-shire, Cromarty's Regiment. Imprisoned Inverness, June 1746 prison ship *Wallsgrave*, Tilbury. Transported 19.3.1747 from Tilbury. *SHS.3.130, MR85.*

McKENZIE, KENNETH, aged 20, from Inverness, Cromarty's Regiment. Imprisoned Inverness, June 1746 prison ship *Alexander & James*, Tilbury. Fate unknown, probably died. *SHS.3.120*.

McKENZIE, MARY, aged 20, spinner from Lochaber, Inverness-shire, "lusty healthy lass, knits and spins." Taken prisoner at capture of Carlisle, 30.12.1745. Imprisoned Carlisle, Lancaster Castle. Transported 5 May 1747 from Liverpool to Leeward Islands in *Veteran*, arriving Martinique June 1747. *SHS.1.217, SHS.3.130, PRO.SP36.102*.

McKENZIE, MURDOCH, aged 20, herdsman in Tully, Dingwall, Sutherland, Cromarty's Regiment. Imprisoned Inverness, June 1746 prison ship *Jane of Leith*, Tilbury Fort. Transported 31.3.1747 from London to Barbados in *Frere*. *SHS.3.130, MR85, BMHS.30.82*.

McKENZIE, MURDOCH, aged 22, servant to Format McLeod, Ross-shire, Cromarty's Regiment. Imprisoned Inverness, June 1746 prison ship *Jane of Leith*, Tilbury Fort. Transported 31.3.1747 from London to Jamaica in *St George or Carteret*, arriving Jamaica 1747. *SHS.3.130, MR85, PRO.CO137.58, BMHS.30.82*.

McKENZIE, MURDOCH, aged 40, farmer in Strath na Calliach, Ross-shire, Cromarty's Regiment. Imprisoned Inverness, June 1746 prison ships *Thane of Fife, James & Mary*. Transported 31.3.1747 from London to Barbados in *Frere*. *SHS.3.130, MR85, BMHS.30.82*.

McKENZIE, RODERICK, aged 30, from Cromarty, Lieutenant, Cromarty's Regiment. Imprisoned Inverness, June 1746 prison ship *Thane of Fife*, Southwark. Acquitted. At his trial he pleaded duress and was acquitted on that ground. *SHS.3.132*.

McKENZIE, RODERICK, aged 26, servant to the Minister of Lochbroom, Cromarty's Regiment. Imprisoned Inverness, June 1746 hospital ship *Liberty & Property*, Medway. Transported 31.3.1747 from London to Jamaica in *St George or Carteret*, arriving Jamaica 1747. *SHS.3.132, MR85, PRO.CO137.58, BMHS.30.82*.

McKENZIE, RODERICK or ROGER, aged 56, husbandry in Logie, Caithness, Cromarty's Regiment. Imprisoned Inverness, June 1746 prison ships *Thane of Fife, James & Mary, Medway*. Transported 31.3.1747 from London to Jamaica in *St George or Carteret*, arriving Jamaica 1747. *SHS.3.132, PRO.CO.137.58*.

McKENZIE, RODERICK, aged 36, farmer in Lochbroom, Ross-shire, Cromarty's Regiment. Imprisoned Inverness, June 1746 prison ship *Liberty & Property*, Medway. Transported 20.3.1747. *SHS.3.132, MR85.*

McKENZIE, RODERICK, aged 40, farmer in Batralliach, Ross-shire, Cromarty's Regiment. Imprisoned Inverness, June 1746 prison ships *Thane of Fife, Liberty*, Medway. Transported 20.3.1747. *SHS.3.132.*

McKENZIE, RODERICK, aged 50, husbandman in the lands of McKenzie of Auchterdonald, Ross-shire, Cromarty's Regiment. Imprisoned Inverness, June 1746 prison ships *Thane of Fife, Liberty*, Medway. Died. *SHS.3.132.*

McKENZIE, RORY, aged 56, husbandman in Little Strath, Ross-shire, Cromarty's Regiment. Imprisoned Inverness, Tilbury. Transported 20.3.1747. *SHS.3.132, MR85.*

McKENZIE, RORY, aged 26, from Ross-shire, Cromarty's Regiment. Imprisoned Inverness, June 1746 prison ship *Alexander & James*, Tilbury Fort. Transported 20.3.1747. *SHS.3.134, MR85.*

McKENZIE, RORY or RODERICK, aged 23, husbandman from Strath na Cailliach, Ross-shire, Cromarty's Regiment. Imprisoned Inverness, June 1746 hospital ship *Liberty & Property*, Medway. Transported 1747. *SHS.3.134, MR85.*

McKENZIE, RORY, aged 23, from Ross-shire, Cromarty's Regiment. Imprisoned Inverness, June 1746 prison ship *Alexander & James*. Fate unknown. *SHS.3.134.*

McKENZIE, SIMON, aged 26, from Inverness, Roy Stuart's Regiment. Imprisoned Carlisle, Lancaster Castle, York Castle. Executed Yortk 8.11.1746. He pleaded guilty at his trial at York on 2 October and was sentenced to death. *SHS.3.134.*

McKENZIE, WILLIAM, aged 25, from Inverness, Duke of Perth's Regiment. Imprisoned Inverness May 1746, prison ship *Jane of Leith*. Died 3.6.1746.

McKENZIE, WILLIAM, aged 26, from Ross-shire, Lieutenant, Cromarty's Regiment. Imprisoned Inverness, June 1746 prison ship *Thane of Fife*, Southwark. Nothing more is known of him. *SHS.3.134.*

McKENZIE, WILLIAM, aged 30, from Ross-shire, Cromarty's Regiment. Imprisoned Inverness, June 1746 prison ship *Thane of Fife*, Tilbury. Nothing more is known of him. *SHS.3.134.*

McKENZIE, WILLIAM, aged 36, from Ross-shire, husbandman near Banff, Cromarty's Regiment. Imprisoned Inverness, June 1746 prison ships *Thane of Fife, James & Mary, Medway*. Transported 1747. *SHS.3.134, MR85.*

McKENZIE, WILLIAM, aged 21, from Ross-shire, Cromarty's Regiment. Imprisoned Inverness, June 1746 prison ship *Alexander & James*. Transported 1747. *SHS.3.136, MR85.*

McKINNON, ANGUS, from Skye, Clanranald's Regiment. Imprisoned Tilbury. Released. Turned King's Evidence. *SHS.3.136.*

McKINNON, ANNE, Lady, Clanranald's Regiment. Imprisoned Morar; London (in messenger's house). Released 4.7.1747. Wife of John Mackinnon of Mackinnon. She was taken prisoner to London along with her husband. On 25 May 1747 the Privy Council decided she was to be released on bail, "No evidence appearing against her." *SHS.3.136.*

McKINNON, DONALD, farmer from Clatill, Isle of Egg, Clanranald's Regiment. Imprisoned Sept 1746, HMS *Pamela*, Tilbury. Was not transported, probably died. *SHS.3.136.*

McKINNON, DONALD, from Skye, Clanranald's Regiment. Imprisoned Inverness, Tilbury. Transported 31.3.1747 from London to Barbados, in *Frere*. *SHS.3.136, MR143, BMHS.30.82.*

McKINNON, HECTOR, "rebel service" imprisoned Fort Augustus June 1746. Hanged 29.6.1746. Deserter from Lord Loudoun's Highlanders; captured at Fort Augustus. *SHS.3.136.*

MacKINNON, JOHN, of MacKinnon, aged 70, Strath, Skye, McKinnon's (Keppoch) Regiment. Imprisoned 11.7.1746 Morar, Inverness, Tilbury, London, Southwark (in house of a messenger, Mr Munie), Released January 1749-50. The old Chief, John Mackinnon, had been out in the '15, but was pardoned. He joined the Prince on 13 October 1745 with 120 men and served through the campaign. He was the only one of the three chiefs in Skye who went out. He was not at Culloden, as he had been sent to Sutherland in pursuit of Lord Loudoun's force. The Prince went to him in Skye in July 1746, and Mackinnon helped him to reach the mainland. He was arrested on 11 July 1746 in Morar, and taken to London, where it was decided he should be tried at Carlisle or Derby. This, however, was not carried out, and on 19 Jan

1749/50 he petitioned for release, saying he was old, "destitute of all funds except a small allowance from the Government," and "never yet examined or anything laid to his charge." He was probably released shortly afterwards. He died 7 May 1756. *SHS.1.294, SHS.3.136.*

McKINNON, JOHN, of Ellagol (Elgol), Skye, McKinnon's Regiment. Imprisoned 11.7.1746 Elgol, HMS *Furnace*, Oct 1746 Tilbury, Southward. Released 3.7.1747. Nephew of John Mackinnon of Mackinnon, the Chief, with whom he served through the campaign. In company with his Chief he helped the Prince to escape from Skye to the mainland in July 1746. He was caught on 11 July and put on board ship, where he was examined by General Campbell as to his reasons for not giving up the Prince and earning the reward. When he replied that he would not have done it for the whole world the officers rose and drank to his health. He was ordered to be transported, but must have been reprieved. He was in hospital in Edinburgh in 1761 paralysed in both legs, and he died 11 May 1762 in Bath. *SHS.3.138.*

McKINNON or McKININ, NEIL, tailor. Imprisoned "on suspicion" Edinburgh Castle, 23.1.1746 Edinburgh Jail, discharged sick 23.2.1746. *SHS.3.138.*

McKINNON, or McKINNON, NORMAN, McKinnon's Regiment. Imprisoned 22.11.1745 Edinburgh Jail. Liberated 3.12.1745. "A common man on suspicion." *SHS.3.138.*

McKISSOCK or McKESSOGG (MacISAIC), DUNCAN, aged 20, Clanranald's Regiment. Imprisoned Inverness June 1746, prison ship *Liberty*, Tilbury. Transported 20.3.1747 from Tilbury. *SHS.3.138, MR143.*

McLACHLAN, ALEXANDER, from Ladhill, Argyllshire, Major, Duke of Atholl's Regiment. Imprisoned Inverness, June 1746 prison ship *Jane of Leith* Tilbury, London (Southwark). Escaped 22.10.1748. "Tidewaiter in the Port of Fort William." "Made Major in the Rebel army, was taken and sent to London prisoner." This was the Major McLachlan who was so tightly handcuffed that "his hands swell'd so that the irons could not be seen." He was kept in this condition for ten days. At his rial in London on 6 November 1746 he was convicted and sentenced to death with a recommendation to mercy. His name appears among those to be transported, but he was still in prison in October 1748, when he escaped. *SHS.3.138.*

McLACHLAN, ALEXANDER, from Fort William, Argyllshire. Imprisoned Carlisle 30.12.1745. Acquitted 19.9.1746. Taken at capture of Carlisle. Was tried there on 19 Sept 1746 and acquitted. SHS.3.140.

McLACHLAN, ARCHIBALD, merchant in Maryburgh, from Argyllshire. Imprisoned 17.3.1746 Edinburgh Castle, 8.8.1746 Carlisle. This may have been the "Lachlan Dow," servant to Allan Mclachlan, who turned King's Evidence in London against Mackinnon of Mackinnon. SHS.3.140.

McLACHLAN, COLIN, from Argyllshire. Imprisoned on Holy Island, Edinburgh Castle, 15.1.1746 Edinburgh Jail. Nothing is known of him except that in the Jail returns he is described as a "Surgeon from Jamaica." "Says that he was not concerned in the rebellion." He was arrested on suspicion. The State Records say that "there is full proof against Colin McLachlan, that he came twice to Gosford commanding a body of armed Highlanders during the time the rebel army was in this country, in quest of Mr John Wedderburn, Gosford's son, who it is alleged debauched his sister." SHS.1.219, SHS.3.140.

McLACHLAN, DOUGAL, aged 59, husbandman from Argyllshire, ander." On suspicion. McLachlan's Regiment. Imprisoned 3.11.1746 Blackness, Edinburgh Castle, 15.1.1746 Edinburgh, 8.8.1746 Carlisle. Transported 1747. "A common highlander." On suspicion. "Leading a blind man when caught." SHS.3.140, MR181.

McLACHLAN, PETER, tacksman of Lettermore, Mull. Imprisoned 9.6.1746 Dumbarton. Discharged 18.7.1747. Capt Millar of Guise's Regiment went to his house and burnt and plundered everything he had. "There is proof of his being in arms with the rebels." SHS.4.142.

MacLACHLAN, LAUCHLAN, of Castle Lachlan, killed at Culloden SHS.1.294.

McLAURIN or McLAREN, DONALD, drover from Western Invernentie, Balquhidder, Captain, Appin Stewart's Regiment. Imprisoned 19.7.1746 Braes of Leny; Stirling, Edinburgh, Canongate. Escaped Aug 1746. He was captured, with some others, while living in a hut in the Braes of Leny. Defending himself he was wounded in the thigh. "When on his way to Carlisle strapped to a dragoon, he cut the strap, threw himself over a cliff and escaped. This incident occurred on Erickstane Brae at the hollow formerly called Annandale's Beefstand but now McLaren's Leap."

After his escape he went back to his own country and remained in disguise until the Act of indmenity. *SHS.3.142.*

McLEAN, ALEXANDER, Pedlar from Inverness area, Duke of Atholl's Regiment. Imprisoned Winsley, Cheshire, Chester Castle, York Castle. Transported 1747. At his trial, 2 Oct 1746, he pleaded guilty and was sentenced to death, but reprieved. *SHS.3.144, MR25.*

McLEAN, ALEXANDER, aged 40 from Ross-shire, Cromarty's Regiment. Imprisoned Inverness, June 1746 prison ship *Jane of Leith*, Tilbury. Transported 20.3.1747 from tilbury to Jamaica in *St George or Carteret*, arriving Jamaica 1747. *SHS.3.144, MR85, PRO.CO137.58.*

McLEAN, ALEXANDER, aged 25, from Lochbroom, Cromarty's Regiment. Imprisoned Inverness, Tilbury Fort. Was not transported; probably died. This may have been the man about whom his minister sent a petition showing he was forced and surrendered. *SHS.3.144.*

McLEAN, ALLAN, from Tiree, McLean of Drimnin's Regiment. Imprisoned Aug 1746 Tiree, Dumbarton Castle, 4.2.1747 Glasgow. Discharged 15.7.1747. "Was with rebels 4 days and knows not the regiment." *SHS.3.144.*

McLEAN, ALLAN DOW, from Tiree, McLean of Drimnin's Regiment. Imprisoned Aug 1746 Tiree, Dumbarton Castle, 4.2.1747 Glasgow. Discharged. "Was with rebels 4 days and knows not the regiment." *SHS.3.144.*

McLEAN, ANGUS, aged 43, farmer from Island of Eigg, Clanranald's Regiment. Imprisoned Inverness, prison ship *Pamela*, Tilbury. Transported 31.3.1747 from London to Jamaica in *St George or Carteret*, arriving Jamaica 1747. *SHS.3.144, MR143, PRO.CO137.58, BMHS.30.82.*

McLEAN, ARCHIBALD, from Balemartine, Tiree, McLean of Drimnins Regiment. Imprisoned Aug 1746 Tiree, Dumbarton Castle, 4.2.1747 Glasgow. Discharged 15.7.1747. "Says he was not with rebels." "Was recruiting men in company with McLean of Drimnin, and when the Duke of Argyle's factor went to the country to raise the Militia openly opposed him and threatened to mob him. Apprenhended by a part sent by General Campbell." *SHS.3.144.*

McLEAN, ARCHIBALD, from Sendaig, Tiree, McLean of Drimnins Regiment. Imprisoned Aug 1746 Tiree, Dumbarton Castle, 4.2.1747 Glasgow. Discharged 15.7.1747. "Says he was not with rebels." "Was recruiting men in company with

McLean of Drimnin, and when the Duke of Argyle's factor went to the country to raise the Militia openly opposed him and threatened to mob him. Apprenhended by a part sent by General Campbell." *SHS.3.144.*

McLEAN, ARCHIBALD, from Skye, Clanranald's Regiment. Imprisoned 13.1.1746 Linlithgow, 20.1.1746 Leith, 7.2.1746 Edinburgh, 8.8.1746 Carlisle. Nothing more is known of him. He may have died, as his name does not appear on the transportation lists. *SHS.3.144.*

McLEAN, DANIEL, from Argyll. Imprisoned Perth. Discharged 29.3.1746. Servant to Mr James Stewart, "minister in Kilbrand, Argyllshire." On suspicion. Accused of carrying treasonable letters. One of these contained "some rebellious lines or verses." *SHS.3.146.*

McLEAN, DONALD, from South Uist, Clanranald's Regiment. Imprisoned Dumbarton Castle, Glasgow. Discharged. "Acknowledges that he received arms from the rebels, but denies that he was doing battle with them." *SHS.3.146.*

McLEAN, DONALD, from Inverness-shire, Glengarry's Regiment. Imprisoned 4.11.1745 Duddingston, Edinburgh Castle, 15.1.1746 Edinburgh. Discharged. He was probably a deserter from the Regiment. *SHS.3.146.*

McLEAN, DOUGAL, aged 16, Ross-shire, labourer, Cromarty, Mackintosh's Regiment. Imprisoned Inverness, June 1746 prison ship *Jane of Alloway*, Tilbury Fort. Transported 31.3.1747 from London to Barbados in *Frere*. *SHS.3.146, MR177, BMHS.30.82.*

McLEAN, DUNCAN, aged 42, farmer in Dornie, Ross-shire, Cromarty's Regiment. Imprisoned Inverness, June 1747 prison ship *Jane of Leith*, Tilbury Fort. Transported 31.3.1747 from London to Barbados in *Frere*. *SHS.3.146, MR85, BMHS.30.82.*

McLEAN, FARQUHAR, from Ross-shire, Cromarty's Regiment. Imprisoned Inverness, June 1746 prison ship *James & Mary*. Transported 31.3.1747 from London to Jamaica in *St George or Carteret*, arriving Jamaica 1747. *SHS.3.146, MR85, PRO.CO137.58.*

McLEAN, or MACLEAN of DUART, Mull, Sir HECTOR, Bart, Major, Lord John Drummond's Regiment. Imprisoned 5.6.1745 Edinburgh, London (Newgate). Discharged 9.4.1747 and delivered into the hands of a messenger. Finally released Juen 1747. Arrested "on suspicion of enlisting men for the French service." According to Forbes,

John Blaw of Castlehill said Sir Hector came over from France in June 1745 with a message from the Prince to the Duke of Perth. Shortly after his arrival he was arrested on 5 June 1745 and incriminating documents were found on him, addressed to the Duke of Perth and Murray of Broughton, and was taken to London. Sir Hector was tried for his life on the charge of being in the French service and of raising men for it, but, on proving that he had been born in Calais, he was treated as a prisoner of war. He appears to have been in prison for two and a half years. *SHS.3.148.*

McLEAN, HECTOR, aged 44, farmer in Langwell, Ross-shire, Cromarty's Regiment. Imprisoned Inverness, Tilbury Fort. Transported 31.3.1747 from London to Barbados in *Frere*. *SHS.3.148, MR85, BMHS.30.82.*

McLEAN, HECTOR, aged 40, from Cromarty, Cromarty's Regiment. Imprisoned Inverness, June 1746 prison ship *Jane of Leith*, Tilbury. Transported 20.3.1747 from Tilbury. *SHS.3.148, MR85.*

McLEAN, HECTOR, from Tiree, McLean of Drimnin's Regiment. Imprisoned Aug 1746 Tiree, Dumbarton Castle, 4.2.1747 Glasgow. Discharged 15.4.1747. "Servant to James Reid." "Forced out into the rebellion by his said master." Denies he was in any service or regiment. "Ferried with his boat 19 men from Tiree to join the rebels, went with them and was at the battle of Culloden in McLean of Drimnin's corps. *SHS.3.148.*

McLEAN, JOHN, cook to Clanranald, and cooked for the Prince while on the Long Island. Imprisoned HMS *Furnace*, London. Became Evidence against Clanranald. Discharged. *SHS.3.148.*

McLEAN, JOHN, aged 16, labourer from Argyll, McLachlan's Regiment. Imprisoned Inverness, June 1747 prison ship *Jane of Alloway*, Tilbury Fort. Transported 31.3.1747 from London to Jamaica, in *St George or Carteret*, arriving Jamaica 1747. *SHS.3.148, MR181, PRO.CO.137.58, BMHS.30.82.*

McLEAN, JOHN, aged 25, Clanranald's Regiment. Imprisoned Inverness, Tilbury. Transported from Tilbury. *SHS.3.148, MR144.*

McLEAN, JOHN, gardener at Laagg, Island of Eigg, Clanranald's Regiment. Imprisoned June 1746 *Jane of Alloway*, Sept 1746 prison ship *Pamela*, Tilbury. Transported 1747. *SHS.3.148, MR144.*

McLEAN, JOHN, from Killcrew, Isle of Skye, Sergeant, Duke of
Perth's Regiment. Imprisoned Canongate, Carlisle,
7.2.1746 Coventry, York Castle. Executed York 8.11.1746.
"Denies that he was in rebellion. Can give no distinct
account of himself. Guilty of habitual stealing." At his trial
at York on 2 October he pleaded guilty and was sentenced to
death. *SHS.4.150.*
McLEAN, JOHN, of Kenway, Tiree, Mclean of Drimnin's Regiment.
Imprisoned Aug 1746 Tiree, Aug 1746 Dumbarton Castle,
4.2.1747 Glasgow. Discharged 15.7.1747. "Knows not in
whose regiment, being as he says 4 days with the rebels."
As a matter of fact in company with other McLeans he was
recruiting in the island and was molested by the Duke of
Argyle's factor. Having threatened to mob him they were
apprehended. See Archibald McLean, Balemartine,
Sendaig. *SHS.3.150.*
McLEAN, JOHN, of Icolmkill (Iona). Imprisoned 6.3.1746/7
Edinburgh Castle, London, house of Dick, the messenger.
Released 10.6.1747. "Gentleman." "There is full proof of
his piloting a Spanish ship from Icolmkill to Barra in October
or November 1745, and that he administered oaths to
several persons whereby they were to swear that she
belonged to England, though he had told them before that
she was for the Pretender's service." This incident refers to
the Spanish ship which landed £4000 and 2500 stand or
arms in Barra. *SHS.3.150.*
McLEAN, LACHLAN, servant to Sir Hector McLean, Bt of Duart.
Imprisoned 5.6.1745 Canongate, Londong (Newgate).
Released June 1747. He was with his master when the
latter was arrested in June 1745 and was himself taken
prisoner. He was in Newgate until June 1747, when he was
released under the Act of Pardon. *SHS.3.150.*
McLEAN, MALCOLM, bricklayer, aged 17. Imprisoned Carlisle.
Transported from Liverpool to Maryland in *Gildart*, arriving
Port North Potomac, Maryland 5 Aug 1747. *SHS.3.150,
PRO.T1.328.*
McLEAN, NEILL, from Tiree, McLean of Drimnin's Regiment.
Imprisoned Aug 1746 Tiree, Aug 1746 Dumbarton Castle,
4.2.1747 Glasgow. Discharged 15.7.1747. *SHS.3.150.*
McLEAN, THOMAS, aged 25, from Auchterlintor, Ross-shire,
Cromarty's Regiment. Imprisoned Inverness, June 1746
prison ship *Jane of Leith*, Tilbury Fort. Transported
31.3.1747 from London to Barbados in *Frere.* Servant to

Murdoch McKenzie of Auchter Lintor. *SHS.3.152, MR85, BMHS.30.82.*
McLEAN, or MACKLAIN, WILLIAM, tailor from Ruthven, Badenoch, Inverness-shire. Imprisoned 3.2.1746 Doune Castle, 13.2.1746 Leith. Released under General Pardon, 1747. *SHS.3.152.*
McLEAN, WILLIAM, bricklayer from Lorn. Imprisoned 25.2.1746 Stirling Castle. Released under General Pardon, 1747. *SHS.3.152.*
McLEAN, WILLIAM, aged 32, labourer from Inverness-shire. Imprisoned Carlisle, York Castle. Transported Antigua 8.5.1747 to Leeward Islands in *Veteran*, arriving Martinique June 1747. *HS.3.152, PRO.SP36.102.*
McLEAN, WILLIAM, aged 14, from Lochbroom, Cromarty's Regiment. Imprisoned Inverness, June 1746 prison ship *Thane of Fife*, Tilbury. Transported from Tilbury. His minister appealed for him as having been forced. *SHS.3.152, MR86.*
McLEARE, ALEXANDER, aged 26, farmer in Achnahard, Lochbroom, Ross-shire, Cromarty's Regiment. Imprisoned Inverness, Tilbury. No reference to his being transported, probably died. *SHS.3.152.*
McLELLAN (or McCLELLAND), DONALD. Imprisoned Inverness, prison ship *Alexander & James*. Died 19.5.1746. *SHS.3.154.*
McLENNAN, ALEXANDER, aged 16, cowherd, Glenmoriston, Inverness-shire, Glengarry's Regiment. Imprisoned September 1746, prison ship *Pamela*, Tilbury. No reference to his being transported; may have died. But his parish minister appealed for him and he may have been released. *SHS.3.152.*
McLENNAN (McGLENAN), ALEXANDER, aged 28, blacksmith from Agherahard, Lochbroom, Ross-shire, Cromarty's Regiment. Imprisoned Inverness, Tilbury Fort. No reference to his being transported; may have died. *SHS.3.154.*
McLENNAN, ANGUS, aged 33, farmer, Burblach, Morar, Inverness-shire, Glengarry's Regiment. Imprisoned Inverness Sept 1746, prison ship *Pamela,* Tilbury. Transported 31.3.1747 from London to Barbados in *Frere. SHS.3.154, MR158, BMHS.30.82.*
McLENNAN, ANGUS, farmer, Morar, Inverness-shire, Glengarry's Regiment. Imprisoned Inverness, Sept 1746 prison ship

Pamela, Tilbury. Transported 20.3.1747 from Tilbury. *SHS.3.154, MR158.*

McLENNAN, ANGUS, Inverness-shire, Glengarry's Regiment. Imprisoned Inverness, prison ship *Pamela*, Tilbury. Transported 31.3.1747. *SHS.3.154.*

McLENNAN, DONALD, farmer, Burblach, Morar, Inverness-shire, Glengarry's Regiment. Imprisoned Inverness, prison ship *Pamela*, Tilbury. Transported 31.3.1747 from London to Barbados in *Frere*. *SHS.3.154, MR159, BMHS.30.82.*

McLENNAN, DONALD, farmer, Killconan, Glengarry, Inverness-shire, Glengarry's Regiment. Imprisoned Inverness Sept 1746, prison ship *Pamela*, Tilbury. Transported 20.3.1747 from Tilbury. "A bad man." *SHS.3.154, MR159.*

McLENNAN, DONALD, farmer, Morar, Inverness-shire, Glengarry's Regiment. Imprisoned Sept 1746, prison ship *Pamela*, Tilbury. Not transported, may have died. *SHS.3.154.*

McLENNAN, DUNCAN, aged 43, dairyman to McKenzie of Corry, Ross-shire. Cromarty's Regiment. Imprisoned Inverness June 1746, prison ship *Jane of Leith*, Tilbury Fort. Transported 20.3.1747 from London to Barbados in *Frere*. *SHS.3.154. MR86, BMHS.30.82.*

McLENNAN, FARQUHAR, aged 38, farmer at Burt, Glengarry, Inverness-shire. Glengarry's Regiment, Imprisoned Sept 1746 prison ship *Pamela*, Tilbury, Hospital Ship. Transported 1747 from Tilbury. A surgeon. *SHS.3.154, MR159, BMHS.30.82.*

McLELLAN or McCALLUM or McLENNAN, JOHN, from Inverness-shire, Glengyle's Regiment. Imprisoned 9.11.1745 Ardno, 17.12.1745 Dumbarton. Liberated 21.8.1747. *SHS.3.154.*

McLENNAN, JOHN, aged 33, from Inverness-shire. "Tayloring in the country. Club Feet." Glengarry's Regiment. Taken prisoner after Culloden. Imprisoned Inverness June 1746, prison ship *Mary & James*, Tilbury. Transported 31.3.1747. *SHS.1.234, SHS.3.156, BMHS.30.82.*

McLENNAN, ROBERT, aged 25, from Ross-shire, Cromarty's Regiment. Imprisoned Inverness, June 1746 prison ship *Jane of Leith*. Fate unknown; probably died. *SHS.3.156.*

McLENNAN, RODERICK or RORY, aged 25, farmer, Aghtascaild, Ross-shire, Cromarty's Regiment. Imprisoned Inverness, Tilbury Fort. Transported 31.3.1747 from London to Barbados in *Frere*. *SHS.3.156, MR86, BMHS.30.82.*

McLEOD, ALEXANDER, son of John Macleod, advocate, escaped. SHS.1.295.

McLEOD, ALEXANDER, aged 50, husbandman, Dingwall, Ross-shire, Cromarty's Regiment. Imprisoned Inverness, June 1746 prison ship *Jane of Lieth*, Tilbury Fort. Transported 20.3.1747 from Tilbury. SHS.3.156, MR86, BMHS.30.82.

McLEOD, ALEXANDER, aged 26, farmer, Kerogarregh, Lochbroom, Ross-shire, Cromarty's Regiment. Imprisoned Inverness, June 1746 prison ship *Jane of Leith*, Tilbury Fort. Transported 31.3.1747 from London to Jamaica in *St George or Carteret*, arriving Jamaica 1747. SHS.3.156, MR86, PRO.CO137.58, BMHS.30.83.

McLEOD, ALEXANDER, aged 40 (34), ploughman to Mr McCowlah, from Lochbroom, Ross-shire, Cromarty's Regiment. Imprisoned Inverness, June 1746 prison ship *Wallsgrave*, Tilbury Fort. Transported 1747 from Tilbury. SHS.3.156, MR86.

McLEOD, ALEXANDER, aged 18, labourer from Inverness-shire, Glengarry's Regiment. Imprisoned Carlisle, York Castle. Transported 19.3.1747. SHS.3.156.

McLEOD, ALEXANDER, aged 18, labourer from Inverness-shire, Glengarry's Regiment. Imprisoned Carlisle, York Castle. Transported 19.3.1747. SHS.3.156.

McLEOD, ALEXANDER, aged 19, labourer from Inverness-shire. Transported 5 May 1747 from Liverpool to Leeward Islands, in *Veteran*, arriving Martinique June 1716. SHS.3.156, MR159, PRO.SP36.102.

McLEOD, ANGUS, aged 35, labourer from Inverness-shire, Glengarry's Regiment. Imprisoned Carlisle, York Castle. Transported from Liverpool to Virginia in *Johnson*, arriving Port Oxford, Maryland, 5 Aug 1747. SHS.3.156, MR159, PRO.T1.328.

McLEOD, DANIEL, aged 36, from Inverness-shire, Lovat's Regiment. Imprisoned Inverness, June 1746 prison ship *Margaret & Mary*. Not transported; may have died. SHS.3.158.

McLEOD, DANIEL, aged 44, from Ross-shire, Cromarty's Regiment. Imprisoned Inverness, prison ship *Liberty*, Tilbury. Transported 31.3.1747 from London to Barbadoes, in *Frere*. SHS.3.158, MR86.

McLEOD, DONALD, aged 68, from Gualtergil, Dunvegan, Skye, Glengarry's Regiment. Imprisoned 5.7.1746 Benbecula; Portree, HMS *Furnace*, 9.8.1746 London (Tilbury), prison ship *Jane of Leith*, House of a messenger. This was one of the most faithful of all the Prince's attendants. He was sent to the Prince at Borrodale on 21 April 1746 by Aeneas Macdonald, and offered to help him to get over to the Hebrides in the hopes of picking up a ship for Frances. He got a boat and crew and took him across, and shared his adventures until 20 June, when the small party had to scatter to avoid detection. On 5 July he was captured by Allan McDonald of Knock, taken to Barra and thence to Portree, and put on board Ferguson's ship. He was taken to Tilbury and put in a prison ship, where he suffered appalling ill-treatment. For some months he was in the house of Mr Dick the messenger. He was never tried, and he himself never referred to any official examination. In the absence of sufficient evidence he was released 10 June 1747 and went home, dying there in May 1749, aged 72. His wife was sister of McDonald of Borrodale, and first cousin of Flora McDonald. *SHS.1.227, SHS.3.158.*

McLEOD, DONALD, Glengarry's Regiment. Imprisoned Inverness, died on prison ship *Alexander & James*, 17 May 1746. *SHS.1.188, SHS.3.160.*

McLEOD, DONALD, aged 44, farmer in Coigach, Ross-shire, Cromarty's Regiment. Imprisoned Inverness June 1746, prison ships *Alexander & James*; *Liberty & Property* Medway. Transported 20.3.1747 from London to Jamaica in *St George or Carteret*, arriving Jamaica 1747. *SHS.3.158, MR86, PRO.CO137.58, BMHS.30.83.*

McLEOD, DONALD, aged 22, servant to Alexander McLeod, Coigach, Ross-shire, Cromarty's Regiment. Imprisoned Inverness, June 1746 prison ship *Wallsgrave*, Tilbury Fort. Transported 31.3.1747 from London to Jamaica in *St George or Carteret*, arriving Jamaica 1747. *SHS.3.158, MR86, PRO.CO137.58, BMHS.30.83.*

McLEOD, DONALD, aged 26, farmer in Croshill, Ross-shire, Lovat's Regiment. Imprisoned Inverness June 1746 prison ship *Liberty*, Medway. Transported 31.3.1747 from London to Jamaica, in *St George or Carteret*, arriving Jamaica 1747. *SHS.3.158, MR86, PRO.CO137.58, BMHS.30.83.*

McLEOD, DOUGAL, aged 50, from Argyll, Clanranald's Regiment. Imprisoned Culloden, Inverness June 1746, prison ship *Thane of Fife*, Tilbury. Nothing more is known of him; he may have died. *SHS.3.160.*

McLEOD, DUNCAN, aged 24, from Cromarty, Cromarty's Regiment. Imprisoned Inverness, June 1746 prison ship *Jane of Leith*. Transported 20.3.1747. *SHS.3.160, MR86*.

McLEOD, DUNCAN, aged 19, from Inverness-shire, Cromarty's Regiment. Imprisoned Inverness, June 1746 prison ships *Margaret & Mary, James & Mary*, Tilbury Fort. Transported 31.3.1747. Deserter from Loudoun's Regiment. Servant to an officer in that regiment. Said to have been "taken by the rebels," ie forced. *SHS.3.160, MR86*.

McLEOD, DUNCAN, aged 23, from Ross-shire, Cromarty's Regiment. Imprisoned Inverness, June 1746 prison ship *Jane of Leith*. Transported 20.3.1747. *SHS.3.160*.

McLEOD, HUGH, miller from "Shigareth", Inverness-shire, Glengarry's Regiment. Imprisoned Carlisle, Chester Castle. Drowned at Liverpool when going on board a ship for transportation, 2 May 1747 (or March 1747). *SHS.1.188, SHS.3.160*.

MacLEOD, Lord JOHN MACKENZIE, aged 19 from Dunrobin. Imprisoned 1746 Dunrobin; Tower of London. Conditional pardon 22.1.1748. Eldest son of the 3rd Earl of Cromartie; was born 1727. Along with his father he took part in the '45. This was not expected, as the Lord President had offered him a commission as Captain of one of the Independent Companies. He raised a body of Mackenzies in Lochbroom and Coigach and joined the Prince on the return of the army from the English campaign. He and his father, Barisdale, Glengyle, and Mackinnon were sent with 1500 men to try to recover the treasure on the *Prince Charles* (ex *Hazard*) which had been driven ashore at Tongue, on 25 March 1746, and to raise money in Sutherland and Caithness. They were surprised and captured at Dunrobin and taken to London, and a large number of their men were taken prisoners. When tried for high treason on 20 Dec 1746 Lord Macleod pleaded guilty. He was pardoned on 22 Jan 1748 on condition that within six months of attaining his majority he should convey to the Crown all his rights in the Estates of the Earldom. This he did, and went abroad and entered the Swedish service, becoming a Colonel. He returned home in 1777 and raised the "Macleod Highlanders," with which he served in India. The family estates were returned to him by Act of Parliament in 1784. He died in 1789. *SHS.3.160*.

McLEOD, JOHN, aged 40, from Glenelg. Imprisoned Sept 1746, prison ship *Pamela* Tilbury. Transported 31.3.1747 from

London to Jamaica in *St George or Carteret*, arriving
Jamaica 1747. "Cook to Lady Barra in the Isle of Barra."
SHS.3.162, PRO.CO137.58, BMHS.30.83.

McLEOD, JOHN, aged 57, farmer, Ullabell (Ullapool), Lochbroom,
Ross-shire, Cromarty's Regiment. Imprisoned Inverness,
June 1746 prison ship *Jane of Leith*, Tilbury Fort.
Transported 31.3.1747 from London to Barbados in *Frere.*
SHS.3.162, MR86, BMHS.30.83.

McLEOD, JOHN, aged 41, farmer in Dormy, Ross-shire,
Cromarty's Regiment. Imprisoned Inverness, June 1746
prison ship *Jane of Leith*, Tilbury Fort. Transported
20.3.1747 from Tilbury. *SHS.3.162, MR86, BMHS.30.83.*

McLEOD, JOHN, aged 18, herded cattle in Budschall, Ross-shire,
Cromarty's Regiment. Imprisoned Inverness, June 1746
prison ship *Jane of Leith*, Tilbury Fort. Transported
31.3.1747 from London to Jamaica in *St George or Carteret*,
arriving Jamaica 1747. *SHS.3.162, MR86, PRO.CO137.58,
BMHS.30.83.*

McLEOD, JOHN, aged 21, servant to McKenzie of Langwell,
Lochbroom, Ross-shire, Cromarty's Regiment. Imprisoned
Inverness, June 1746 *Jane of Leith*, Tilbury Fort.
Transported 31.3.1747 from London to Jamaica in *St George
or Carteret*, arriving Jamaica 1747. *SHS.3.162, MR86,
PRO.CO137.58, BMHS.30.83.*

McLEOD, JOHN, aged 25, labourer from Inverness-shire,
Cromarty's Regiment. Imprisoned Carlisle, York Castle.
Transported Antigua 8.5.1747, from Liverpool to Leeward
Islands, in *Veteran*, arriving Martinique June 1747.
SHS.3.162, MR86, PRO.SP36.102.

McLEOD, JOHN, aged 24, from Inverness-shire. Imprisoned
Inverness, June 1747 prison ship *Jane of Alloway*, Tilbury.
Was not transported; probably died at Tilbury. *SHS.3.162.*

MacLEOD of Brea, Captain MALCOLM rom Raasay. Imprisoned
July 1746 Raasay, Portree; Tilbury, Ldondon (Mr Dick's
house). Released 4.7.1747. Capt Macleod met the fugitive
Prince at Portree on 30 June 1746 and took him to Raasay.
They left on 2 July and returned to Skye and went to Strath,
the Prince posing as his servant. Here they were in the
house of John Mackinnon, Macleod's brother in law.
Macleod returned to Raasay, where he was taken prisoner
and placed on a sloop commanded by the barbarous John
Ferguson and conveyed to London. For several months he
was in one of the prison ships at Tilbury. On 25 May 1747

the Privy Council decided he should be tried in Scotland, but this was not carried out. He was ultimately released on 4 July 1747 and returned home. *SHS.3.164.*

McLEOD, MURDOCH, aged 18, from Ross-shire. Herdsman to Kenneth McKenzie of Asson. "Follower of the rebel army." Cromarty's Regiment. Imprisoned Inverness, June 1746 prison ship *Jane of Leith*, Tilbury Fort. Transported 31.3.1747 from London to Barbados in *Frere. SHS.3.164, MR86, BMHS.30.83.*

McLEOD, MURDOCH, aged 21, from Ross-shire. Servant to Duncan Simpson of Ferintosh. Cromarty's Regiment. Imprisoned Inverness, June 1747 prison ship *Jane of Leith*, Tilbury Fort. Transported 31.3.1747 from London to Jamaica in *St George or Carteret*, arriving Jamaica 1747. *SHS.3.164, MR86, PRO.CO137.58, BMHS.30.83.*

McLEOD, MURDOCH, aged 45, from Inverness-shire. Farmer in Skye, Glengarry's Regiment. Imprisoned Inverness, June 1747 prison ships *Alexander & James, Liberty*, Medway. Transported 31.3.1747 from London to Barbados in *Frere. SHS.3.166, MR159, BMHS.30.83.*

McLEOD, NEIL, aged 21, husbandman at Hillach, Isle of Raasay, McLeod of Raasay's Regiment. Imprisoned Invernes, prison ship *Pamela*, Tilbury. Transported 20.3.1747 from London to Jamaica in *St George or Carteret*, arriving Jamaica 1747. *SHS.3.166, MR185, PRO.CO137.58, BMHS.30.83.*

McLEOD, RODERICK or RORY, aged 20, from Ross-shire, Cromarty's Regiment. Imprisoned Inverness, June 1746, prison ship *Jane of Leith*, Tilbury Fort. Lived with his father in Langwell. Transported 31.3.1747 from London to Jamaica in *St George or Carteret*, arriving Jamaica 1747. *SHS.3.166, MR86, PRO.CO137.58, BMHS.30.83.*

McLEOD, SAUNDERS, aged 55, Cromarty's Regiment. Imprisoned Inverness, Tilbury Fort. Transported 31.3.1747. SHS.3.166, MR86.

McMARTIN, ANGUS, aged 20, Clanranald's Regiment. Imprisoned Inverness, June 1746 prison ship *Pamela*, Tilbury. Transported 31.3.1747 from London to Barbados in *Frere. SHS.3.168, MR144, BMHS.30.83.*

McMARTIN, ANGUS, aged 18, cowherd from Kirktown, Isle of Eigg, Clanranald's Regiment. Imprisoned Inverness, June 1746 prison ship *Pamela*, Tilbury. Transported 31.3.1747 from London to Jamaica in *St George or Carteret*, arriving

Jamaica 1747. *SHS.3.168, MR144, PRO.CO137.58, BMHS.30.83.*

McMARTIN, MALCOLM, aged 60, from Inverness-shire, Lochiel's Regiment. Imprisoned Inverness, June 1746 prison ship *Pamela*, Tilbury. No reference to having been transported, probably died. *SHS.3.168, BMHS.30.83.*

McMASTER, MALCOLM, aged 50, husbandman from Fort William, Inverness-shire. Imprisoned on suspicion Inverness, June 1746 prison ship *Liberty*, Medway. Transported 31.3.1747 from London to Jamaica on *St George or Carteret*, arriving Jamaica 1747. *SHS.3.168, PRO.CO137.58.*

McMASTER, WILLIAM, aged 60, from Argyllshire. Imprisoned on suspicion Inverness, June 1746 prison ship *Margaret & Mary*. *SHS.3.168.*

McMILLAN or McMULLEN, ARCHIBALD, aged 32, servant to Ewen Cameron of Glenfean, Argyll, Lochiel's Regiment. Imprisoned Inverness, June 1746 prison ship *Wallsgrave*, Tilbury Fort. *SHS.3.168.*

McMILLAN or McMULLEN, DONALD, aged 30, from Sheuglie, Glenurquhart, Inverness-shire, Glengarry's Regiment. Imprisoned Inverness, June 1746 prison ship *Alexander & James*. Transported 1747. Wounded after Culloden, but rescued by a man from Lochaber. He was one of the few who escaped from abroad and returned home. He was known in after life as the "Grey Smith of Inchvalgar." *SHS.3.168, MR159.*

McMILLAR, DONALD, imprisoned prison ship *Alexander & James*, died 8.6.1746. *SHS.3.168.*

McMILNE, ARCHIBALD, from Argyll, Duke of Perth's Regiment. Imprisoned 30.12.1745 Carlisle. Taken at capture of Carlisle. Fate not known. *SHS.3.168.*

McMUDIE, LACHLAN, imprisoned Tilbury. Released. Turned King's Evidence against Allan McDonald, chaplain of Clanranald's. *SHS.3.168.*

McMURICH or MACPHERSON, or McMURRAY, ALAN (LACHLAN), aged 39, farmer from Galmistal, Isle of Eigg, Clanranald's Regiment. Imprisoned Inverness, June 1746 prison ship *Pamela*, Tilbury. Evidence against Clanranald. Transported 31.3.1747 from London to Jamaica on *St George or Carteret*, arriving Jamaica 1747. *SHS.3.168, MR144, PRO.CO137.58, BMHS.30.83.*

McNAUGHTON, DUNCAN, from Argyllshire. "Servant to him called Duke of Perth." Imprisoned 23.4.1746 North

Queensferry, 23.4.1746 Dunfermline. Liberated 6.3.1747. *SHS.3.170.*

McNEAL, GEORGE, aged 35, from Caithness, Cromarty's Regiment. Imprisoned Inverness, June 1746 prison ship *Thane of Fife*, Tilbury. Not shown as transported, probably died. *SHS.3.172.*

McNEILL or McNEIL, DUNCAN, imprisoned 15.12.1745 Ardno, 17.12.1745 Dumbarton. Escaped 2.2.1746. *SHS.3.172.*

McNEIL, DUNCAN, from Lochaber. "A common highlander" from Lochaber, Glengyle's Regiment. "Miner at Wanlockhead. Denies that he was in arms or any way assiting to the rebels." Liberated 10.3.1746. *SHS.3.172.*

McNEILL or McKNEAL, RODERICK or ROGER, of Barra. He was aged 53, from Isle of Barra. Imprisoned July 1746 Inverness, prison ship *Pamela*, Tilbury Fort, London. Discharged 28.5.1747. Although he took no part in the Rising he was arrested on suspicion and taken to London in July 1746. He turned King's Evidence. He was released the following year. *SHS.3.174.*

McNEIL, ROGER, aged 28, "servant" from Isle of Barra, Clanranald's Regiment. Imprisoned 1746, prison ship *Pamela* Tilbury. Lived with the Laird at Watersay in Barra. Transported from Tilbury. *SHS.3.174, MR144.*

McNICOL, RONALD, chapman from Glenorchy, Glengyle's Regiment. Imprisoned 15.11.1745 Ardno, 17.12.1745 Dumbarton. Liberated 5.8.1747. *SHS.3.174.*

McOWEN or McEWEN, CATHERINE, aged 40, from Fort William, Inverness-shire. Imprisoned 30.12.1745 Carlisle, Lancaster Castle. Taken at capture of Carlisle. Transported 1747. *SHS.1.217, SHS.3.174.*

McPHADEN, ALLAN, from Mull. Discharged. "Denies that he was in the rebellion. Can give no distinct account of himself. Guilty of habitual stealing." *SHS.3.174.*

McPHEE, EWEN or OWEN, aged 28, from Locharkaig, Lochiel's Regiment. Imprisoned Inverness, Sept 1746 prison ship *Pamela* Tilbury. Servant to Donald Cameron of Clunes. Transported 31.3.1747 from London to Barbados in *Frere*. *SHS.3.174, MR36, BMHS.30.83.*

McPHEE, HUGH (or EWEN), aged 30, labourer from Inverness-shire. Imprisoned Lancaster Castle. Transported Antigua 8.5.1747. *SHS.3.174.*

McPHEE, MURDOCH, aged 43, from Morven, Argyll, farmer Sandvegg, Eigg, Clanranald's Regiment. Imprisoned

Inverness Sept 1746 *Pamela*, Tilbury. Transported 31.3.1747 from London to Jamaica in *St George or Carteret*, arriving Jamaica 1747. *SHS.3.174, PRO.CO137.58, MR144, BMHS.30.83.*

McPHERSON, ALEXANDER, labourer from Strathspey, Keppoch's Regiment. Imprisoned 6.11.1745 Dalkeith, 25.1.1746 Edinburgh Jail. Released under General Pardon, 1747. *SHS.3.176.*

McPHERSON, ANGUS, from Kinlochmoidart, servant to Kinlochmoidart, Clanranald's Regiment. Imprisoned Nov 1745 Lesmahagow, Edinburgh. Released under General Pardon, 1747. "Says he had not been above three days in Kinlochmoidart's service when he was taken along with his master, and that he never saw the rebel army." This shows that McPherson was with his master on the latter's unsuccessful mission to Sir Alexander McDonald of Sleat, and was caught with him at Lesmahagow. *SHS.3.176.*

McPHERSON, ANGUS (or AENEAS), drover from Strathnairn, Inverness-shire, Clanranald's Regiment. Imprisoned Douglas, 15.1.1746 Edinburgh Castle, Edinburgh Tolbooth. Discharged. "Denies that he was concerned with the rebels." He was sick in hospital with fever in June 1746. *SHS.3.176.*

McPHERSON, ARCHIBALD, aged 16, cowherd from Skye, Clanranald's Regiment. Imprisoned 30.12.1745 Carlisle, York Castle, Lincoln Castle. Taken at capture of Carlisle. Transported Antigua 8.5.1747 from Liverpool to Leeward Islands, in *Veteran*, arriving Martinique June 1747. *SHS.3.176, MR144, PRO.SP36.102.*

McPHERSON, DONALD, from Moidart, Clanranald's Regiment. Imprisoned 7.11.1747 Kelso, Edinburgh 12.8.1746 Canongate. Released under General Pardon, 1747. *SHS.3.176.*

McPHERSON, DUNCAN, aged 36, labourer from Inverness-shire, Glenbucket's Regiment. Imprisoned Carlisle, York Castle. Transported Antigua 8.5.1747 from Liverpool to Leeward Islands, in *Veteran*, arriving Martinique June 1747. *SHS.3.176, MR123, PRO.SP36.102.*

McPHERSON, JOHN, aged 43, servant from Inverness-shire, McIntosh's Regiment. Imprisoned Inverness, June 1746 prison ship *Dolphin*, Tilbury Fort. Transported 31.3.1747 from London to Barbados in *Frere*. *SHS.3.176, MR177, BMHS.30.83.*

McPHERSON, JOHN, aged 15, from Glengarry, Inverness-shire, Glengarry's Regiment. Imprisoned 4.1.1746 Newcastle, Carlisle, Chester Castle. Transported 24.2.1747 from Liverpool to Virginia in *Gildart*, arriving Port North Potomac, Maryland, 5.8.1747. *SHS.3.178, MR159, PRO.T1.328.*

McPHERSON, KENNETH, Merchant drover from Ruthven, Inverness-shire. Imprisoned Edinburgh Castle, Bathgate, 15.1.1746 Edinburgh Jail from Castle. Liberated 10.5.1746. An officer in rebel service. *SHS.3.178.*

McQUARRY, or McQUIRRY, ALEXANDER, aged 37, from Morven, Argyll, farmer at Fivepenny, Eigg, Clanranald's Regiment. Imprisoned Inverness, Sept 1747 *Pamela* Tilbury. Transported 20.3.1747 from Tilbury. *SHS.3.178, MR144.*

McQUARRY, DONALD, from Island of Eigg, Clanranald's Regiment. Imprisoned Sept 1746 prison ship *Pamela*, Tilbury. Transported 31.3.1747 from London to Barbados in *Frere*. *SHS.3.178, MR144, BMHS.30.83.*

McQUARRY, or McQUIRY, DONALD, aged 25, Clanranald's Regiment. Imprisoned 17.3.1746 Edinburgh Castle, Tilbury. Transported 20.3.1747. *SHS.3.178.*

McQUARRY (McQUARRISH), JOHN, from Island of Eigg, farmer at Galmistill, Eigg, Clanranald's Regiment. Imprisoned Sept 1746 prison ship *Pamela*, Tilbury. Transported 31.3.1747 from London to Barbados in *Frere*. *SHS.3.178, MR144.*

McQUARRY, DONALD, from Island of Eigg, Clanranald's Regiment. Imprisoned Sept 1746 *Pamela*, Tilbury. Transported 31.3.1747 from London to Barbados in *Frere*. *SHS.3.178, MR144, BMHS.30.83.*

McQUARRY, (McQUARRISH), JOHN, Clanranald's Regiment. Imprisoned Inverness, Tilbury. Transported 1747. *SHS.3.178.*

McQUARRY, JOHN, from Eigg, Clanranald's Regiment. Imprisoned Inverness, Tilbury. Transported 1747. *SHS.3.178.*

McQUARRY, or McQUIRRY, JOHN, aged 40, from Eigg, Clanranald's Regiment. Imprisoned Inverness, Tilbury. Transported 1747. *SHS.3.178, MR144.*

McQUARRIE or McWARISH or McALQUARISH, JOHN, from Moidart, "surgeon, rebel service," Clandranald's Regiment. Imprisoned 7.11.1745 Kelso, Edinburgh Castle, 15.1.1746 Edinburgh, 12.8.1746 Canongate. Released under General Pardon, 1747. *SHS.3.180.*

McQUARRIE or McWARISH or McALQUARISH, JOHN, servant to John McAlquarish, surgeon," Clandranald's Regiment. Imprisoned 7.11.1745 Kelso, Edinburgh Castle, 15.1.1746 Edinburgh, 12.8.1746 Canongate. Released under General Pardon, 1747. *SHS.3.180.*

McQUEEN, ANGUS, from Isle of Skye, servant to McLeod of Raasay, McLeod of Raasay's Regiment. Imprisoned Inverness Sept 1746, prison ship *Pamela* Tilbury. Transported 20.3.1747. *SHS.3.180, MR185.*

McQUEEN, or MacQUEEN, JOHN, from Inverness-shire, Glenbucket's Regiment. Imprisoned 30.12.1745 Carlisle, York Castle. Taken at capture of Carlisle. Pleaded guilty at his trial and was sentenced to death, 2 October 1746. He was reprieved. Ultimate fate not known. *SHS.3.180.*

McQUERRIST, JOHN, imprisoned Carlisle, Liverpool. Transported 22.4.1747 from Liverpool to Virginia in *Johnson*, arriving Port Oxford, Maryland 5.8.1747. *SHS.3.180, PRO.T1.328.*

McQUERRIST, RODERICK, imprisoned Carlisle, Liverpool. Transported 22.4.1747 from Liverpool to Virginia in *Johnson*, arriving Port Oxford, Maryland 5.8.1747. *SHS.3.180, PRO.T1.328.*

McQUILLY, DONALD, farmer, Howlin, Island of Eigg, Clanranald's Regiment. Imprisoned Inverness, Sept 1746 prison ship *Pamela*, Tilbury. *SHS.3.180.*

McQUIN, ANGUS, aged 24, McLeod of Raasay's Regiment. Imprisoned Inverness, prison ship *Pamela*. Nothing more known of him; probably died. *SHS.3.180.*

McQUIN, FLORA, from the "Highlands." Imprisoned Lancaster Castle. Transported 22.4.1747 from Liverpool to Virginia in *Johnson*, arriving Port Oxford, Maryland, 5.8.1747. *SHS.1.217, SHS.3.180, PRO.T1.328.*

McQUIN, JOHN, imprisoned Carlisle; York Castle. Pardoned on condition of enlistment 22.7.1748. "Taken in actual rebellion. Pleaded at his trial on 2 Oct 1746 and was sentenced to death, but reprieved. *SHS.3.180.*

McRAE or McCRAW, ALEXANDER, from Inverness-shire, Cromarty's Regiment. Imprisoned Sept 1746, prison ship *Pamela*, Tilbury. Cowherd to John Fraser at Muirtown. Not transported; may have died. *SHS.3.182.*

MACRAE or McCRAW, DONALD, from Inverness-shire, Cromarty's Regiment. Imprisoned prison ship *Alexander & James*. Died at sea 24.5.1746. *SHS.1.188, SHS.3.182.*

MACRAE or McCRAW, DONALD, from Inverness-shire, Cromarty's Regiment. Imprisoned prison ship *Alexander & James*. Died at sea 9.6.1746. *SHS.1.188, SHS.3.182.*

MACRAE or McCRAW, DONALD, from Lochbroom, Glengarry's Regiment. Imprisoned Tilbury. An appeal was submitted for him by his Minister, but without avail. Transported from Tilbury to Jamaica in *St George or Carteret*, arriving Jamaica 1747. *SHS.3.182, MR159, PRO.CO137.58.*

McQUARRY, DONALD, from Island of Eigg, Clanranald's Regiment. Imprisoned Sept 1746 *Pamela*, Tilbury. Transported 31.3.1747 from London to Barbados in *Frere*. *SHS.3.178, MR144, BMHS.30.83.*

McRA or McRAW, MURDOCH, from Kintail. Imprisoned May 1746 Inverness. Hanged as a spy, Inverness, May 1746. Spoken of as "nearest relation to the chieftain of that name." He was captured by a party at the house of McDonald of Leek, and although he had taken no part in the Rising was sent to the Duke of Cumberland in Inverness. Here he was immediately hanged as a spy, protesting his innocence. *SHS.3.182.*

McRANALD, DONALD, Clanranald's Regiment. Imprisoned Inverness, Tilbury. Transported from Tilbury. *SHS.3.182, MR144.*

McRAW, DONALD (or RORY), aged 24, farmer from Clochgowrie, Ross-shire, Cromarty's Regiment. Imprisoned Inverness, June 1746 prison ship *Liberty*, Tilbury. Transported 20.3.1747. *SHS.3.182, MR87.*

McRAW or McRARS, RORY, aged 21, from Ross-shire, Cromarty's Regiment. Imprisoned Inverness, June 1746 prison ship *Alexander & James*. Nothing more is known of him, probably died. *SHS.3.184.*

McRIEVRE, DUNCAN, from Benbecula. One of the Prince's Boatmen. Imprisoned HMS *Furnace*, Tilbury. "For having rowed the Pretender's son from South Uist to Skye." No further reference to him – or released. *SHS.1.227, SHS.3.184.*

McRORY, DONALD, from Lochbroom, Cromarty's Regiment. Imprisoned Tilbury. A petition was put in for him by Rev James Robertson. Fate unknown. *SHS.3.184.*

McRORY, TASKEL, aged 62, from Inverness-shire, Cromarty's Regiment. Imprisoned Inverness, June 1746 prison ship *Alexander & James*. Probably died, as he was not transported. *SHS.3.184.*

McROSS, DONALD, aged 24, from Sutherland. Cromarty's Regiment. Imprisoned Inverness, June 1746, prison ship *Alexander & James*. Transported 1747. *SHS.3.184, MR187*.

McSWANE, ANGUS, aged 20, from Ross-shire, Cromarty's Regiment. Imprisoned Inverness, Tilbury Fort. Servant to John McLeod in Belmore. Fate unknown; probably died. *SHS.3.184*.

McSWEENE, ANGUS, aged 62, farmer in Roach, Isle of Skye, Lovat's Regiment. Imprisoned Inverness June 1746, prison ship *Jane of Alloway*, Tilbury Fort. Not transported; probably died. *SHS.3.184*.

McTAVISH, DUGALD of Dunardary, Argyllshire. Imprisoned Dumbarton. Released under General Pardon, 1747. "Apprehended by warrant from the Deputy Lieutenants of Argyleshire for treasonable practise. His case appears from four letters found upon Sir James Campbell which McTavish acknowledged were of his hand writing." *SHS.3.184*.

McVANE or McWEAN, JOHN, aged 20, from Inverness-shire, McGillivray of Dunmaglass (McIntosh's) Regiment. Imprisoned Inverness June 1746, prison ship *Jane of Alloway*, Tilbury Fort. Servant to Jno. McFarlane in Petty. Fate unknown; not transported; probably died. *SHS.3.184*.

McVANNAN, JOHN, aged 26, from Isle of Skye, Glengarry's Regiment. Imprisoned Inverness; Tilbury Fort. Servant to Angus McDonald in Turting. Fate unknown, not transported, probably died. *SHS.3.184*.

McVURICH (or McWARISH), LACHLAN, from Moidart, one of the Prince's Boatmen, made prisoner for helping the Prince to escape to Uist. Imprisoned London, in house of Dick the messenger. Released 10.6.1747 after turning King's Evidence against Lady Clanranald. *SHS.1.227, SHS.3.186*.

McVURRISH or McOURICH or McWARISH, MALCOLM, from Balemcanoch, Tiree, McLean of Drimnin's Regiment. Imprisoned Tiree, 4.2.1747 Glasgow. Discharged 15.7.1747.

McWARISH, JOHN, doctor, Inverness, surrendered and released. *SHS.1.220*.

McWILLIAM, JOHN, from Kilmorack, Inverness-shire, Cromary's Regiment. Imprisoned prison ship *Alexander & James*. Died at sea. 27.5.1746. "Was with the rebels and taken prisoner." *SHS.1.188,* SHS.3.186.

McVANNAN, JOHN, aged 26, from Isle of Skye, Glengarry's Regiment. Imprisoned Inverness; Tilbury Fort. Servant to Angus McDonald in Turting. Fate unknown, not transported, probably died. SHS.3.184.

McVURICH (or McWARISH), LACHLAN, from Moidart, one of the Prince's Boatmen, made prisoner for helping the Prince to escape to Uist. Imprisoned London, in house of Dick the messenger. Released 10.6.1747 after turning King's Evidence against Lady Clanranald. SHS.1.227, SHS.3.186.

McVURRISH or McOURICH or McWARISH, MALCOLM, from Balemcanoch, Tiree, McLean of Drimnin's Regiment. Imprisoned Tiree, 4.2.1747 Glasgow. Discharged 15.7.1747.

REIRIE or REIRY or RHEEDY, DAVID, aged 20, father in the land of the laird of Latheren, Caithness, Cromarty's Regiment. Imprisoned Inverness Sept 1746, prison ship *James & Mary* Tilbury. Transported 30.3.1747. SHS.3.270, MR87.

RICHIE or RYTCHIE, WILLIAM, aged 18, from Inverness-shire. Transported 31.3.1747 from London to Jamaica in *St George or Carteret*, arriving Jamaica 1747. SHS.3.274, MR75, PRO.CO137.58, BHMS.84.

RIDDEL or RIDDLE, JOHN, from Inverness-shire, groom to Lord Lovat. Imprisoned London. Discharged. "Was in the battle of Culloden and soon after surrendered." He turned King's Evidence against Lord Lovat. He said that, after the battle of Prestonpans, he saw 500 Frasers "drawn up on the green at Castledownie, but could not tell whether my Lord Lovat knew of it." This man is specially mentioned in the Duke of Cumberland's Instructions to David Bruce, Judge Advocate, as to be "taken care of." SHS.3.272.

RINKEI (sic), WILLIAM, aged 18, from Inverness-shire, in "Rebel Service". Imprisoned Inverness, prison ship *Liberty*. Was servant to the King's surgeon, Fort St George. As he was not transported he may have died. SHS.3.272.

RITCHIE, WILLIAM, aged 18 from Inverness-shire, Duke of Perth's Regiment. Imprisoned prison ships *Thane of Fife, Pamela,* Tilbury. Transported 31.3.1747 from London to Jamaica, in *St George or Carteret*, arriving Jamaica 1747. SHS.3.274, MR75, PRO.CO137.58.

ROBERTSON, JOHN, aged 19, labourer from Inverness-shire. Imprisoned Lancaster Castle, York Castle. Transported Antigua 8.5.1747 from Liverpool to Leeward Islands in

Veteran, arriving Martinique June 1747. *SHS.3.278, PRO.SP36.102.*

ROSE, HUGH, aged 41, farmer in Fottertie, Ross-shire, Cromarty's Regiment. Imprisoned Inverness, Tilbury Fort. No further reference to him. Does not appear in transportation list. May have died. *SHS.3.284.*

ROSE, THOMAS, from Inverness, Lord George Murray's Regiment. Imprisoned 30.12.1745 Carlisle. Taken at capture of Carlisle. No further reference to him. Does not appear in transportation list. May have died. *SHS.3.284.*

ROSS, ALEXANDER, aged 20, from Carrol Clyne, Sutherland, Lord George Murray's (Duke of Atholl) Regiment. Imprisoned Inverness, June 1746 prison ship *Thane of Fife*, Tilbury, 1.11.1746 Southwark. Servant to Gordon of Carroll. Transported 1747. *SHS.3.286, MR27.*

ROSS, ALEXANDER, aged 17, from Ross-shire, Clanranald's Regiment. Imprisoned inverness, June 1746 prison ship *Thane of Fife*. No further reference to him. *SHS.3.286.*

ROSS, ALEXANDER, aged 50, farmer in Kirktown of Lochbroom, Ross-shire, Cromarty's Regiment. Imprisoned Inverness June 1746, prison ship *Alexander & James*, Tilbury. Transported 31.3.1747 from London to Jamiaca, in *St George or Carteret,* arrived Jamaica 1747. *SHS.3.286, MR87, PRO.CO.137.58, BHMS.84.*

ROSS, ANGUS (alias McWilliam), from Tain, Cromarty's Regiment. Imprisoned Inverness. Pardoned. "Now enlisted in the Master of Ross his company." This appears to indicate that he was captured after Culloden and accepted enlistment in Lord Loudoun's regiment, in the company commanded by William, Master of Ross, as an alternative to transportation. *SHS.3.286.*

ROSS, DANIEL, aged 26, from Inverness-shire, Roy Stuart's Regiment. Imprisoned Inverness, June 1746 prison ship *Margaret & Mary*. No further reference to him. May have died. *SHS.3.286.*

ROSS, DANIEL, aged 56 from Inverness. Imprisoned Inverness, June 1746 prison ship *Wallsgrave,* Tilbury Fort. Taken on suspicion. Mason at Redcastle. No further reference to him. May have died. *SHS.3.286.*

ROSS, DANIEL, aged 20, servant to Hector McKenzie, Ross-shire, Cromarty's Regiment. Imprisoned Inverness, June 1746 prison ship *Jane of Leith*, Tilbury Fort. No further reference to him. May have died. *SHS.3.286.*

ROSS, DANIEL, aged 40, from Ross-shire. Imprisoned York
Castle. "Taken in actual rebellion." Transported Antigua
8.5.1747 from Liverpool to Leeward Islands in *Veteran*,
arriving Martinique June 1747. *SHS.3.286, PRO.SP36.102.*

ROSS, DAVID, from Ross-shire. Imprisoned 20.6.1746 Dundee.
Discharged 16.3.1747. "Common man." Suspicion of
treason. *SHS.3.288.*

ROSS, DONALD, aged 56, Cromarty's Regiment. Imprisoned
Inverness, Tilbury Fort. Transported 31.3.1747 from London
to Jamaica in *St George or Carteret*, arriving Jamaica 1747.
SHS.3.288, MR87, PRO.CO137.58.

ROSS, DONALD, aged 20, Cromarty's Regiment. Imprisoned
Inverness, Tilbury Fort. Transported 20.3.1747 from Tilbury.
SHS.3.288, MR87.

ROSS, DONALD, aged 24, from Inverness-shire, Roy Stuart's
Regiment. Imprisoned Inverness Sept 1746, prison ship
James & Mary, Tilbury. Servant to Joseph Stewart of
Cromar, a rebel. Transported 20.3.1747 from Tilbury.
SHS.3.288, MR207.

ROSS, DUNCAN, aged 30, farmer in Aichennarver, Ross-shire,
Cromarty's Regiment. Imprisoned Inverness, June 1746
prison ship *Jane of Leith*, Tilbury Fort. Transported
31.3.1747 from London to Barbados in *Frere*. *SHS.3.288,
MR87, BHMS.84.*

ROSS, HUGH, aged 40, from Ross-shire, Cromarty's Regiment.
Imprisoned Inverness, June 1746 prison ship *Jane of
Alloway*. No further reference to him. May have died.
SHS.3.288.

ROSS, HUGH, "suspected of being a spy." Imprisoned 14.2.1746
Montrose, 17.3.1746 Edinburgh Castle. Discharged.
SHS.3.288.

ROSS, HUGH, aged 26, farmer in Balavich, Fotterty, Ross-shire,
Stonywood's Regiment. Imprisoned Culloden, Inverness,
June 1746 prison ships *Thane of Fife, James & Mary*
Medway, Southwark. Discharged. Servant to Mr
Thompson of Fifefield. He became Evidence against Adam
Hay of Asslid and others at the trial at Southwark.
SHS.3.288.

ROSS, JOHN, aged 17, miller in Forbloch, Ross-shire, Glengarry's
Regiment. Imprisoned Inverness, June 1746 prison ships
Thane of Fife, Liberty, Medway. Transported 31.3.1747
from London to Jamaica in *St George or Carteret*, arriving

Jamaica 1747. *SHS.3.290, MR159, PRO.CO137.58, BHMS.84.*

ROSS, RONALD or RANDAL, aged 18, husbandman from Miltoun of Ord, Urra, Ross-shire, Cromarty's Regiment. Imprisoned Inverness, June 1746 prison ships *Thane of Fife*, *Liberty*, *Tilbury*. "Was with the rebels and taken prisoner in Sutherland." Transported 31.3.1747 from London to Jamaica, in *St George or Carteret*, arriving Jamaica 1747. *SHS.3.290, MR87, PRO.CO137.58, BHMS.84.*

ROSS, THOMAS, from Tain, Ross-shire, Cromarty's Regiment. Imprisoned Inverness. Pardoned. "Served in Cromarty's rebel regiment, now enlisted in the Master of Ross' his company." This indicates that he enlisted in Loudoun's Regiment to escape transportation. *SHS.3.290.*

RURY, DAVID, aged 20, from Caithness, Cromarty's Regiment. Imprisoned Inverness, June 1746 prison ship *Thane of Fife*. No further reference to him. He may have died. *SHS.3.294.*

SHAW, MARY, aged 40, from Inverness. Imprisoned Carlisle, Lancaster Castle. Transported 22.4.1747 from Liverpool to Virginia in *Johnson*, arriving Port Oxford, Maryland, 5 Aug 1747. *SHS.3.308, PRO.T1.328.*

SHAW, MURDOCH, from Inverness, Mackintosh's Regiment. Imprisoned 1.2.1746 Stirling, 17.3.1746 Edinburgh Castle, 13.12.1746 Edinburgh Jail from Castle. Released under General Pardon, 1747. "Confesses he was servant to Mr McGillivray of Drumnaglass, a rebel officer, and various parties declare he was in the rebellion." Alexander McGillivray was Colonel of Mackintosh's killed at Culloden. *SHS.3.308.*

SIMPSON, JOHN, aged 55, from Caithness, Cromarty's Regiment. Imprisoned Inverness, June 1746 prison ship *Jane of Leith*, Tilbury Fort. Discharged. "Suspected to be a rebel soldier in Lord Loudoun's left sick." This is the man who turned Evidence for the Crown against Lord Lovat. *SHS.3.314.*

SINCLAIR, or St CLAIR, JAMES, aged 19, husbandman in Dunbeith, Caithness, Cromarty's Regiment. Imprisoned Inverness, June 1746 prison ships *Thane of Fife, James & Mary*. Transported 31.3.1747 from London to Jamaica, in *St George or Carteret*, arriving Jamaica 1747. *SHS.3.316, PRO.CO137.58, MR87, BHMS.84.*

SINCLAIR, or St CLAIR, JAMES, aged 20, Cromarty's Regiment. Imprisoned Inverness, June 1746 prison ship *Thane of Fife*.

There is no further reference to him. He may have died. *SHS.3.316.*

SMITH (*alias* McINTOSH), DONALD, labourer from Lochaber, Keppoch McDonald's Regiment. Imprisoned 3.10.1745 Livingston Yards, Edinburgh, Edinburgh Castle, 15.1.1746 Edinburgh Jail. Discharged. "Says the rebels forced him to go the length of Kelso and that he deserted them there." *SHS.3.320.*

SMITH, DONALD, aged 50, from Glen Urquhart, Glengarry's Regiment. Imprisoned Inverness, June 1746 prison ship *Dolphin*. No further reference to him. *SHS.3.320.*

SMITH, JOHN, Elcho's Regiment, died in Edinburgh Castle, 1746 *SHS.1.188.*

STEVEN, GEORGE, aged 13, "baggage bawman (?batman)" from Ross-shire, Cromarty's Regiment. Imprisoned Inverness, June 1746 prison ship *Thane of Fife*. Disposal unknown, may have died. *SHS.3.332.*

STEWART, ALLAN, from Argyllshire, Sergeant. Imprisoned 16.4.1746 Culloden, Inverness, London. Discharged. Son of Dougal Stewart, Maryburgh. "Was a Sergeant in the rebel army, was wounded at Culloden and sent to London." He turned King's Evidence against Major Alex McLachlan and others. *SHS.3.336.*

STEWART, of Burray, Lady ANNE. Imprisoned May 1746 Burray, London, in custody of a messenger, Money. Discharged on bail 4.7.1747. Daughter of David Carmichael of Balmeady, and wife of Sir James Stewart, Bt. of Burray, Orkney. Although she was never tried, the depositions of witnesses showed that she had assisted her husband in trying to get men to join the Prince. She was arrested at the same time as he was, and was sent to London. She appears to have been placed in the custody of Money, a Messenger, on her arrival in London. *SHS.3.338.*

STEWART, CHARLES, of Ardshiel, escaped to France *SHS.1.295*

STEWART, DONALD, "Private man"; his regiment not stated. The only references to him are as in custody of Carrington, the messenger, in June 1748, and as a witness against Aeneas Macdonald and others. Imprisoned Carlisle; London, in house of Carrington, messenger. Released after June 1748. *SHS.3.340.*

STEWART, DUNCAN, aged 21, cattle herd, Breadalbane, from Argyllshire, Roy Stuart's Regiment. Imprisoned Inverness, prison ship *James & Mary*. Transported 1747. *SHS.3.340.*

STEWART, DUNCAN, aged 21, from Argyllshire, Ardshiel's (Appin Stewart's) Regiment. Imprisoned Inverness, June 1746 prison ships *Alexander* & *James, Liberty*, Tilbury. Transported 31.3.1747 from London to Jamaica, in *St George or Carteret*, arriving Jamaica 1747. *SHS.3.342, PRO.CO137.58, BHMS.85.*

STEWART, of Burray, Sir JAMES, Bt. Imprisoned 25.5.1746 Burray, Kirkwall, Stromness, HMS *Shark, Old Loo, Terror*, 7.7.1746 London (Southwark). Died in prison 24.8.1746. Evidences stated that he had been concerned in sending a "Portuguese" (Spanish?) ship in January 1746 from South Ronaldshay to Peterhead, and had done all he could to get men to enlist. He was also seen wearing a white cockade, and was said to be a personal friend of the Prince. The Lord Advocate was very anxious to get a conviction against him. He had taken no active part, but was arrested at his home on 25 May 1746 on suspicion and taken to London. Here he died of fever in the prison at Southwark a few days after he landed, on 24 August 1746. *SHS.3.342.*

STEWART (*alias* McCORMICK), JOHN, tailor from Glencoe "in arms" Appin Regiment. Imprisoned Larbert Bridge, 8.2.1746 Canongate. Discharged 1.1.1747.

STEWART, JOHN, from Balquidder, Inverness-shire "common man" Glengyle's Regiment. Imprisoned 5.7.1746 Perth, 10.8.1746 Canongate. Discharged on bail 30.9.1746. *SHS.3.346.*

STEWART, JOHN, from Ballachulish, Stewart of Ardshiel's Regiment. Imprisoned 21.9.1745 Prestonpans, 22.9.1745 Royal infirmary, Edinburgh, 5.5.1746 Canongate Jail. Released under General Pardon, 1747. Gunshot wound through ankle. *SHS.3.346.*

STEWART, JOHN, aged 14, from Fort Augustus, Glengarry's Regiment. Imprisoned Inverness, Tilbury. Transported 31.3.1747 from London to Barbados in *Frere*. *SHS.3.348, MR160, BHMS.85.*

STUART, DAVID, aged 50, from Ross-shire, Stonywood's Regiment. Imprisoned Inverness, Tilbury Fort. "Lived with George Gordon of Birkenbush, a rebel." Transported 20.3.1747. *SHS.3.340, MR212.*

STUART, DAVID, aged 33, from Ross-shire, Lord Lewis Gordon's Regiment. Imprisoned Inverness, June 1746 prison ship *Wallsgrave*. Discharged. This is apparently the man who turned King's Evidence at the Southwark trials. *SHS.3.340.*

STUART, DOUGAL, from Appin, shoemaker in Edinburgh, Ardshiel's (Stewart's of Appin) Regiment. Imprisoned 21.9.1746 Prestonpans, 22.9.1746 wounded, Prestonpans, and put in Royal Infirmary, Edinburgh 30.3.1746, 25.6.1746 Canongate. Discharged. Taken in arms. Gunshot wound of ankle. "Confesses that he carried arms in the rebel army and was at the battle of Preston, but was forced thereto by Ardshiel." *SHS.3.340.*

STUART, HUGH, aged 58, gardener from Fort Augustus, Inverness-shire, Glengarry's Regiment. Imprisoned Inverness, June 1746 prison ship *Wallsgrave*, Tilbury Fort. Transported 31.3.1747 from London to Barbados in *Frere*. "Says taken on uspicion. Served garrison of Fort Augustus and Captain Romain." *SHS.3.342, MR160, BHMS.85.*

SUTHERLAND, ADAM, aged 56, labourer from Sutherland, Glenbucket's Regiment. Imprisoned 30.12.1745 Carlisle, York Castle, Lincoln Castle. Transported Antigua 8.5.1747 from Liverpool to Leeward islands, in *Veteran*, arriving Martinique June 1747. Taken at capture of Carlisle. *SHS.3.358, MR124, PRO.SP36.102.*

SUTHERLAND, ALAN, aged 19, Cromarty's Regiment. Imprisoned Inverness, HMS *Liberty*, Tilbury. Transported from Tilbury 1747. *SHS.3.358.*

SUTHERLAND, ALEXANDER, aged 40, from Caithness, Cromarty's Regiment. Imprisoned Inverness, June 1746 prison ship *Thane of Fife*. No further reference to him, may have died. *SHS.3.358.*

SUTHERLAND, ALEXANDER, aged 19, husbandman from Ballyhaldrie, Sutherland, Cromarty's Regiment. Imprisoned Inverness, June 1746 prison ships *Thane of Fife, James & Mary, Medway*. Transported 31.3.1747 from London to Barbados in *Frere*. *SHS.3.358, MR88, BHMS.85.*

SUTHERLAND, ALEXANDER, aged 34, from Caithness, sold butter and cheese in Moray, Bannerman's Regiment. Imprisoned Inverness, June 1746 prison ship *Wallsgrave*, Tilbury Fort. Transported 30.3.1747 from London to Jamaica in *St George or Carteret*, arriving Jamaica 1747. *SHS.3.358, MR30, PRO.CO137.58.*

SUTHERLAND, DANIEL, aged 30, from Caithness, Cromarty's Regiment. Imprisoned Inverness, June 1746 prison ship *Thane of Fife*. No further reference to him. *SHS.3.358.*

SUTHERLAND, DANIEL, aged 40, from Caithness, Cromarty's Regiment. Imprisoned Inverness, June 1746 prison ship *Thane of Fife*. No further reference to him. *SHS.3.360*.

SUTHERLAND, JOHN, aged 22, husbandman near Dunbeith, Caithness, Cromarty's Regiment. Imprisoned Inverness, June 1746 prison ships *Thane of Fife, James & Mary, Medway*. Transported 31.3.1747 from London to Jamaica in *St George or Carteret*, arriving Jamaica 1747. *SHS.3.360, MR88, PRO.T1.328, BHMS.85.*

SUTHERLAND, NEIL, aged 35, soldier, from Caithness, Cromarty's Regiment. Imprisoned Inverness, June 1746 prison ship *Jane of Leith*, Tilbury Fort. Transported 31.3.1747 from London to Barbados in *Frere*. Deserter from Lord Loudoun's. "Made prisoner by the rebels; belonged to Lord Loudoun's regiment and was forced into Cromarty's." *SHS.3.360, MR88, BHMS.85.*

SUTHERLAND, WILLIAM, aged 10 (or 13), from Caithness, son of Neil Sutherland (Lord Cromarty's) and Christian Shearer; followed his father. Imprisoned Inverness, June 1746 prison ship *Jane of Leith*, Tilbury Fort. Transported 31.3.1747 from London to Barbados in *Frere*. *SHS.3.360, BHMS.85.*

SUTHERLAND, WILLIAM, aged 30, husbandman in Dunbeith, Caithness, Cromary's Regiment. Imprisoned Inverness, June 1746 prison ship *Thane of Fife, James & Mary, Medway*. Transported 31.3.1747 from London to Jamaica in *St George or Carteret*, arriving Jamaica 1747. *SHS.3.360, MR88, PRO.CO137.58, BHMS.85.*

SWEAN, ANGUS, aged 23 from Inverness-shire. Imprisoned Inverness, June 1746 prison ship *Jane of Alloway*. No further reference to him. *SHS.3.360.*

TAYLOR, DAVID, wright from Inverness. Imprisoned 27.4.1746 Inverness. Released on bail 23.4.1747. On 27 April 1746 he was arrested on suspicion and put in the Tolbooth, which was full of dead and wounded men. On 2 May, he was put in a sloop and sent to Cromarty Road, where he was released. On his return home he was again arrested and incarcerated, and suffered severe hardships. On 23 April 1747 he was released on bail of 1000 merks. "The substance of a long proof against him is that he was a wright to the rebels which some say he did voluntarily, others that he was forced. Likewise he was an overseer of their tradesmen in Inverness.... And that he was in use to attend the non-jurant Episcopal Meeting House. David Gordon heard him wish well to the Pretender's interest." SHS.3.364.

TAYLOR, JAMES, the Rev, aged 52, Episcopal minister from Thurso, Caithness. Imprisoned 25.5.1746 Burray, Kirkwall, HMS Shark, HMS Old Loo, HMS Terror, 7.7.1746 London, Tilbury, HMS Pamela, Tilbury Fort. Released 13.2.1747. In the evidence against Sir James Stewart of Burray it was stated that arms collected for the Prince's army had been concealed in Mr Taylor's house. Shortly after Culloden orders were sent to burn his "meeting house" and to arrest him as a "non-juror." On 25 May he was arrested, along with Sir James Stewart of Burray, and put in a ship and taken to Kirkwall. Thence they were sent to London. In the prison ship Pamela he fell ill and nearly died. After an inquiry into his case it was decided that no charge could be brought against him, and he was released on 13 Feb 1747. SHS.3.364.

TAYLOR, KENNETH, from Lochbroom, Glengarry's Regiment. Imprisoned Tilbury. This man surrendered. His minister petitioned on his behalf that he had been forced out just before Culloden; it is not know, however, whether he was released or died. SHS.3.366.

THOMSON, ANGUS, from Argyll, Roy Stuart's Regiment. Imprisoned 4.11.1745 Bruntsfield Links; 25.1.1746 Edinburgh Jail. Released under General Pardon, 1747. "Soldier." "Late of Col Lee's Regiment. Confesses he was forced to join the rebels after having been confined and ill-used by them, but deserted so soon as he got an opportunity." SHS.3.370.

URQUHART, DONALD, aged 50, blacksmith in Glen Urquhart, Inverness-shire, Glengarry's Regiment. Imprisoned Inverness, Tilbury Fort. Transported 20.3.1747 from Tilbury. SHS.3.382, MR160, BHMS.85.

URQUHART, HECTOR, aged 47, farmer, Aghterneed, Strathpeffer, Ross-shire, Cromarty's Regiment. Imprisoned Inverness, June 1746 prison ship Jane of Leith, Tilbury Fort. Transported 20.3.1747 from Tilbury. SHS.3.382, MR88.

WRIGHT, DUNCAN, aged 40, farmer in Appin, Argyllshire, Roy Stuart's Regiment. Imprisoned Inverness, June 1746 prison ships Alexander & James, Liberty, Medway. Transported 31.3.1747 from London to Jamaica in St George or Carteret, arriving Jamaica 1747. SHS.3.410, PRO.CO137.58, MR207.

YOUNG, MAGNUS, aged 55, from Ross-shire, husbandman near Aberdeen, Farquharson's Regiment. Imprisoned Inverness, June 1746 prison ships *Thane of Fife, James & Mary*. Transported 31.3.1747 from London to Jamaica in *St George or Carteret*, arriving Jamaica 1747. *SHS.3.412, PRO.CO137.58, BHMS.85*.

YOUNG, THOMAS, aged 22, from Ross-shire, Cromarty's Regiment. Imprisoned Inverness, June 1746 prison ship *Wallsgrave*, Tilbury Fort. Lived with his father in Martin, Lochbroom. Transported 31.3.1747 from London to Barbados in *Frere*. *SHS.3.414, MR88, BHMS.85*.

"THE DUMB MAN" alias Keppoch's Dumbie, Keppoch's Regiment. Imprisoned 22.9.1745 Royal Infirmary Edinburgh, 5.5.1746 Canongate. Discharged 6.5.1747. This man, whose name is unknown, was wounded at Prestonpans and suffered gunshot fracture of both bones in one leg. He was placed in the Royal Infirmary, Edinburgh, where he was under treatment until May 1746. When the Prince's army left Edinburgh he was treated as a prisoner. He remained in the Canongate prison until May 1747, when he was discharged. *SHS.3.414.*

www.ingramcontent.com/pod-product-compliance
Lightning Source LLC
Chambersburg PA
CBHW070502090426
42735CB00012B/2653